FEMINIST PEDAGOGY

for Library Instruction

This book is number three in the series Gender and Sexuality in Information Studies, Emily Drabinski, series editor.

Also in the series:

Out Behind the Desk: Workplace Issues for LGBTQ Librarians, edited by Tracy Nectoux.

Make Your Own History: Documenting Feminist and Queer Activism in the 21ˢᵗ Century, edited by Lyz Bly and Kelly Wooten

Forthcoming in the series:

Ephemeral Material: Queering the Archive, by Alana Kumbier

Feminist and Queer Information Studies Reader, edited by Patrick Keilty and Rebecca Dean

Queers Online: LGBT Digital Practices in Libraries, Archives, and Museums, edited by Rachel Wexelbaum

FEMINIST PEDAGOGY

for Library Instruction

by MARIA T. ACCARDI

Library Juice Press
Sacramento, CA

Published by Library Juice Press

PO Box 188784
Sacramento, CA 95818

http://libraryjuicepress.com/

This book is printed on acid-free, sustainably-sourced paper.

Cover design by Jana Vukovic

Library of Congress Cataloging-in-Publication Data

Accardi, Maria T.
 Feminist pedagogy for library instruction / by Maria T. Accardi.
     pages cm. -- (Series on gender and sexuality in information
studies ; number 3)
 Includes bibliographical references and index.
 Summary: "Introduces feminist pedagogy to librarians seeking to
enrich their teaching practices"--Provided by publisher.
 ISBN 978-1-936117-55-0 (alk. paper)
 1. Library orientation for college students. 2. Information literacy-
-Study and teaching (Higher) 3. Research--Methodology--Study
and teaching (Higher) 4. Feminism and higher education. 5.
Critical pedagogy. I. Title.
 Z711.25.C65A27 2013
 025.5'677--dc23
                              2013020013

Contents

Dedication

This book is dedicated to the memory of my first feminist:

Teresa Bisso Marino
1901-1988

From your bella, with love

Acknowledgements

When I was a little girl, I wanted to be a writer. I always believed that I would write a book someday, and now, miraculously, I have. And this childhood dream would never have come true without the support and assistance of a heavenly host of helpers.

Thanks to Rory Litwin for creating a space where a book like this can exist. I thank my editor, Emily Drabinski, for her indefatigable encouragement, nurturing support, and conversations about life and love while petting zoo animals. Her belief in this project helped make it a reality. Thanks to Emily Stenberg for her company, both in person and virtual, during countless coffee shop writing sessions. Thanks to Erin Kate Ryan for decades of fierce and fabulous feminist friendship. Thanks to Tony Mick for his vexing questions on an early draft of this work and for the hilarious voice mails on my work phone. Thanks to Amanda Folk, the best library school BFF a girl could have. Thanks to Quills Coffee and Day's Espresso and Coffee Bar, both of Louisville, Kentucky, for the delicious iced lattes, tasty tea, and free Wi-Fi. Thanks to Mrs. Reidy, the children's librarian at the public library of my childhood, wherever you are, for being the first example of the awesomeness that is librarianship, and also for letting me check out books in the adult section of the library. Thanks to my parents, Philip Accardi and Vicki Thompson, for giving me a typewriter for my 14th birthday, for encouraging my love of reading and writing, and for never, ever telling me to put down that book already. Thanks to my grandmother, Gaetana

Marino Accardi, for serving as an example of unparalleled kindness and generosity. Thank you to Marty Rosen for giving me the time, space, and support to write this book.

And, finally, thank you to the one and only Constance Merritt, who is as steady and unchanging and faithful as her name. Thank you for being my always and everything. ILY.

Maria T. Accardi
Louisville, Kentucky

Introduction

The first time I ever thought about myself as a feminist teacher was when I was a graduate student teaching first year composition at the University of Louisville. In this course, I taught the conventions of formal academic writing through the lens of rhetorical patterns, and as a new teacher who needed a formal structure to guide the class, I required my students to purchase a reader that provided examples of these patterns, such as narration, description, process analysis, comparison and contrast, and so on. Throughout the 15-week semester, I assigned my students to read approximately 40 short essays in this text. Of those 40 essays, perhaps three or four of them had overtly feminist themes.

One such essay was the famous satirical piece "I Want a Wife" by Judy Brady, which originally appeared in *Ms. Magazine* in 1971. When my students read this humorous, tongue-in-cheek examination of the unfair and sexist expectations wives face in heterosexual marriage, we discussed it in class, the way we always did with their readings. There were a series of questions following each essay that were meant to stimulate and provoke discussion. With the classroom desks arranged in a circle, I began the discussion, which typically was dominated by a few people. Getting the rest of the class to talk was difficult. But not so this time. People who never talked in class were moved to speak up about "I Want a Wife." My students were quick to inform me that sexism might have been a problem "back then," but things were great now, and women were equal to men. I was stunned and baffled at their lack of awareness of the continued relevance of feminism, and my efforts to stimulate discussion further on this matter went nowhere, frustrating all of us. Other assigned readings related to sexism, and to racism, faced the same denial and resistance when it came time to examine them in class discussion. In fact, I had one student even assert that there was "no such thing" as African American culture. (The irony that this particular student was herself an immigrant from Africa, and self-identified as Arab, Egyptian, Muslim, and American, was lost on her.) At the end of the semester, I not surprised, but still rather heartbroken, when one of my course evaluations described me as a "feminazi."

If you were to have asked me then, a graduate student in English teaching for the very first time, why I had my students read "I Want a Wife" and other feminist-themed essays, I would have told you that I wanted to raise students' awareness of gender inequity and sexism, and to cultivate a discussion about these issues as a way of examining rhetoric and composition and the conventions of academic writing. Back then, I would not have identified my pedagogical style as explicitly feminist, mostly because I was still finding my identity as a teacher. But as Carolyn Shrewsbury writes (1987), "At its simplest level, feminist pedagogy is concerned with gender justice and overcoming oppressions" (p. 7). This was my instinct as a teacher; that through teaching students about writing I could also raise their consciousness about oppression.

Indeed, I wanted my students to laugh at Brady's sarcastic depiction of the many chores and sacrifices women are expected to make while also arriving at a new understanding of how unjust it was—and is—that women were expected to erase their identities in favor of serving their husbands. And thus I was unknowingly employing feminist pedagogy in the classroom, and apparently, this made me a "feminazi."

This kind of backlash against feminist teaching strategies is certainly not unheard of, and many feminist writers have described the resistance they faced in employing feminist pedagogy in the classroom. Bell, Morrow, and Tastsoglou (1999) observe that students do not always welcome progressive pedagogy, and "instead, they have often resorted to various resistance strategies, ranging from refusal to comply with course requirements to more subtle expressions that appear to undermine our pedagogical efforts" (p. 25). Being accused of being a "feminazi" certainly had an undermining effect on this teacher's confidence, especially a teacher who is still learning how to teach.

Despite my wobbly confidence, I still kept my commitment to the possibilities of feminist teaching practices. As I left the world of teaching writing and transitioned into instruction librarianship, I recalled and retained the philosophies and practices that informed the formation of my identity as a teacher. What gave me hope, what kept me going, what helped me remember that feminist teaching is worth the effort and difficulty, was that even amongst all of my failures and flops, there were shining moments of success.

There was the time I tried decentering myself in the classroom for the first time, refusing to stand in the front of the room, and requiring students to conduct the demonstrations of databases—and found that it successfully facilitated learning in the classroom. There was the first time I conducted research consultations with students that not only dealt with the practical matters of library research but also addressed the affective dimension of research, how students *felt* about the research process—and found that it transformed my relationships with students. There was the first time that I deliberately chose to use a feminist-related topic as a sample search to a class full of students—and found that it awakened my students to a new way of thinking about sexism.

Today, I am no longer a shaky graduate student trying to teach college composition. I am a confident, experienced instruction librarian in a university setting with seven years of college-level teaching to my credit. But I still think of myself as learning how to teach, how to be myself in the classroom while still being a good teacher, and how to face the challenges of feminist teaching within the restricted confines of the traditional 50 to 60-minute one-shot library instruction session.

Today, I am a feminist teacher.

Who is this book for, and why does it matter? My primary intended audience is instruction librarians who teach in college or university settings and who are interested in the possibility of liberatory educational practices. This book will also be of interest to LIS students and faculty in library instruction or information literacy courses. Other college-level instructors and researchers who are involved in progressive pedagogy in general might find this book to be an interesting overview of such practices in the library profession. Feminist scholars and pedagogues will likely find this book to be of interest as I engage and extend our mutual conversations. I wrote this book with these audiences in mind, looking over my shoulder, asking questions, and offering critiques. I hope that these audiences will find that I listened to them and have written a book that they find worth reading.

While I hope to frame theoretical interventions in both library literature and the literature of feminist pedagogy, the primary goal of this book is to provide a theoretical framework and practical guidance for librarians seeking to enrich their pedagogical practices in feminist, progressive ways. It is designed to be a primer: a concise overview of key ideas and principles. It is not intended to be a thorough overview or critique of feminist ideas. This book assumes that feminism is an important and valid lens through which to see the world.

Thus, my approach to defining and exemplifying feminist pedagogy may not be of interest to those who are not feminists or sympathetic to or interested in feminism. Readers seeking more in-depth analyses of feminist ideas may wish to consult the works identified in the literature review in Chapter 2 or the bibliography on page 103.

A secondary goal for this book is to identify and fill a gap in the literature. To date, there is no book-length work or periodical article exploring the connections between library instruction and feminist pedagogy. The only work that I know to exist appears in a book that I co-edited with Emily Drabinski and Alana Kumbier, *Critical Library Instruction: Theories and Methods*, in 2010 from Library Juice Press. This chapter, written by Sharon Ladenson, describes a feminist pedagogy "that resists the banking concept by fostering active learning, and by empowering students to think critically" (p. 105). This book takes inspiration from Ladenson's chapter and seeks to expand on the concepts and techniques she describes there. As I tell the students I work with, when you cannot find articles on your topic, that does not mean your topic is not worth exploring. It just means the literature does not exist yet, and that you have the power to make that literature happen. This is what I am doing here.

Throughout this book, I attempt to demonstrate feminist techniques in action. This book seeks praxis: It takes material form by enacting its own theoretical claims. The book includes personal narratives that illustrate the need for feminist pedagogy and what it looks like in the classroom. While the first person narrative may seem out of place in a book that also attempts to be scholarly, my approach is an intentionally feminist act. The use of the first person destabilizes the centrality of the patriarchal modes of knowledge production that privilege neutrality, objectivity, and as Belenky et al. (1997) observe, "nowhere is the pattern of using male experience to define the human experience seen more clearly than in models of intellectual development" (p. 7). So, in this book, I am using my experience, a white, female, lesbian, cisgender, feminist experience, to produce knowledge and ideas. This book's mere existence is, in short, a feminist act.

Chapter 1 begins by defining feminism through the lenses of narrative, intuition, and experiential knowledge. By employing women's ways of knowing, I outline what feminism means from my own personal epistemological context. Chapter 2 is about pedagogy. Feminist pedagogy is an approach to teaching that is concerned with gender injustice and other inequalities. Through student-centered teaching strategies, feminist teachers seek to raise the consciousness of their students regarding oppression and empower their students to take action. In short, feminist pedagogy is a form of critical pedagogy, which is education for social change. Chapter 3 brings feminist pedagogy in conversation with library instruction theory and practice. By examining current models of information literacy instruction, I argue that the nature of the field leaves it open to feminist critiques. The appendix to this chapter provides concrete examples of feminist pedagogical teaching techniques that can be adopted and modified in the reader's own library instruction classroom. Chapter 4 is about assessment. Where there is teaching, there must also be assessment of that teaching, and feminist approaches to teaching, while progressive, are not immune to this aspect of the dominant culture of higher education.

Now that I've provided you with a brief roadmap of what's to come, here are a few more details to inspire you to read further. In this book, you will learn more about my childhood than you ever realized you wanted to know. You may ask yourself, "What does her childhood have to do with library instruction?" You will, I hope, remain interested enough to keep reading in order to find out. I imagine you, dear reader, interacting with this book. I imagine you laughing at my jokes, scribbling in the margins (although not if it's a library book, of course), and flipping back and forth from the chapters to the Appendix and Further Reading in order to make connections or probe more deeply into the text.

This book represents an intellectual labor of two long years. I hope that this book, the fruit of my heart and mind, will engage you and prompt you to interrogate your own stories, assumptions, beliefs, assertions, and knowledge, while also doing the same to the book itself.

1.

Feminism(s): Narrative, Intuition, and Experiential Knowledge

Gertrude Stein, the lesbian feminist avant-garde writer, instructs us in *Tender Buttons* (1914) to "act so that there is no use in a centre." What does this mean? What she means by this assertion is maddeningly opaque, as is most of *Tender Buttons*, but the reading I choose views "the centre" as patriarchy. Stein is telling us that we need to behave as though the patriarchy, the male-dominated ruling culture, has no use, no power, no control. This does indeed require some acting on our part, because patriarchy is alive and well, oppressing women and queers and other marginalized classes just as usual. And this urging to "act" is worth examining further. This implies action, accomplishment, achievement. This is not a passive exhortation. Rather, it encourages us to be decisive and get going against this thing called the "centre," this thing that oppresses us. This interpretation might be a stretch, but the thing about Stein is that she's not going to come right out and tell you what she thinks. She's going to tell you in a roundabout way. And this oblique rhetoric matches the slanted approach she wants the reader to take. Without a center, we are crooked. We are off-balance. We topple over. Maybe Stein is telling us to topple patriarchy. I take inspiration from Stein's directive in my own assertion that feminism is about, among other things, decentering oppressive power relations and transforming them into something egalitarian and democratic. This includes listening to and creating space for marginalized voices, marginalized ways of being and knowing.

The Western male-dominated majority culture relies on a system of citing that acknowledges the work of others while situating oneself within that scholarly conversation. That is the way the centre would begin this book. But what if I want to write about feminism without situating myself within a scholarly conversation? I want to write about feminism by relying on women's ways of knowing, a way that is off-kilter, as Stein describes. In this section, I will describe feminism as it is conceptualized and operationalized by this book by using feminist strategies: narrative, intuition, and experiential knowledge.[1]

Narrative

Here is a story: My great-grandmother was born in Riesi, Sicily, Italy. We called her Mama Teresa. She came to the United States as a teenager. She married a man who was also from Riesi and who fought in World War I, thus requiring her to depend on her husband for the opportunity of citizenship. When I knew her as a little girl, however, she was dependent on nobody. Rather than having an Old World oppressive relationship, she and Papa Charlie were equals. My childhood perspective on her was that she was thoroughly independent, self-sufficient, wise, and all-knowing. She was ever-present for her children, grandchildren, and great-

---

[1] Some important works that inform my methodology include: Belenky, M. F., Clinchy, B. M., Goldberger, N. R., & Tarule, J. M. (1997). *Women's ways of knowing: The development of self, voice, and mind.* New York: Basic Books; Bergin, L. A. (2002). Testimony, epistemic difference, and privilege: how feminist epistemology can improve our understanding of the communication of knowledge. *Social Epistemology, 16*(3), 197-213; and Lee, J. (1997). Women re-authoring their lives through feminist narrative therapy. *Women & Therapy, 20*(3), 1. See the bibliography and further recommended reading later in this book for more references.

grandchildren, not in a way that erased her selfhood or was self-sacrificing. Her fierce independence, especially after my Papa Charlie died, was significant and awe-inspiring. She never would have called herself a feminist, I don't think, and maybe this is revisionist history for me to think so, but I am telling this story about my Mama Teresa because I think of her as a proto-feminist, my first example of a feminist in my life.

Right up until she died when I was age 11, my Mama Teresa would invite me over to her house to spend the night. She would teach me to cook and bake and clean house. I like to joke that she was teaching me to be a little Italian house-wife, but now I know that she was teaching me to be independent and self-sufficient. She also showed me the importance of taking action to change your circumstances. When I was perhaps seven or eight years old, I had a loose tooth that was bothering me. It was almost, but unbearably not quite, ready to come out. I was at my Mama Teresa's house at a family gathering of some sort, and I suppose that I must have been whining and whimpering about it, because my Mama Teresa took me in hand and led me back to her sewing room. She unwound a length of string and tied one end to the doorknob. She then gestured toward me and made me to understand that she wanted to tie the other end of the string to my loose tooth, at which point she would slam the door, thus pulling out the tooth in question. I quailed at this prospect. I reached into my mouth and pulled out the tooth on my own. Mama Teresa smiled and led me out of the room, poured me a cupful of 7-UP, and I sat quietly for the rest of the evening, gingerly tonguing the freshly emptied space in my mouth, silently marveling at my own audacity.

I think of this story and my Mama Teresa in general when I think about feminism as I understand it. Sexism is agonizing and painful. Feminism acknowledges this pain and takes action to change the circumstances that create and perpetuate it. Even though I opted out of the action Mama Teresa presented to me, it was still impressed upon me the importance of taking practical steps to end your suffering. Feminism, as I believe in it, urges women to state their intentions to bring about change and then follow through to make those changes.

I think I can pinpoint the moment when I became a feminist, but I have to tell you another story in order to explain how this came to be. When I was a child, I wanted to be a writer. I wanted to write stories; I wanted to write poems. And I did write these things. I think what attracted me to writing was the power inherent in storytelling. Stories shape the contours of a life. I grew up on stories of my immigrant ancestors, and I always believed, and was told as much by my relatives, that the story I would write some day would tell my family's story. I am telling my family's story in this book, although this is not how I originally imagined telling these stories.

My great-grandfather, whom we called Papa Charlie, fought for the United States in World War I and thus earned citizenship for himself and his wife, my Mama Teresa. While doing genealogical research during library school, I happened upon a US Census document from 1920, which lists my Papa Charlie's name and information. Under "Whether Able To Read" and "Whether Able To Write," it specifies "NO" and "NO." NO and NO. Does this mean he could not read and write in English? Or that he could not read and write at all?

Papa Charlie died when I was five years old. I don't remember very much about him, but I do remember the children's dictionary he used to learn English. I enjoyed reading his dictionary when visiting him and at some point he gave the dictionary to me. To this day, I still have it. As a little girl, it always struck me as a little odd that Papa Charlie used a children's dictionary to help him learn English, but now, seeing this census record that preserved for all eternity his inability to read or write, it all makes sense.

It is rather staggering to contrast my great-grandfather's lack of basic literacy and my own hyperliteracy. My parents claim that I began reading at age two. I began kindergarten early due to my ability to read. Some of my earliest childhood memories involve libraries. I was always an active participant in my local public library summer reading programs, and the first place I was allowed to go to unaccompanied by an adult was the public library. The library was a safe place, a haven from the chaos of life, a source of solace to a child who tended toward worry and anxiety. I cannot think about the landscape of my childhood without thinking about the library and reading and stories. I learned very early on that stories give life. Stories define and shape what we believe to be true. Stories shape who we are. One story in particular shaped me into a mini-feminist.

Some of the stories I thrived on early were stories of the saints. Raised in the Roman Catholic Church and educated at parochial schools, I was provided with and devoured a series of books about the saints written for young children. I remember being particularly struck by the tale of St. Maria Goretti, a young Italian teenager who was almost raped and then subsequently murdered by her assailant. What made her a saint? Why, her insistence on preserving her virtue, of course. "Death, but not sin," was her cry while her assailant stabbed her multiple times. Yes, it was so important to her to preserve her virginity that she submitted to being stabbed to death instead of submitting to rape. Goretti forgave her murderer before she died, and she then appeared to him in a vision while he was in prison. Her murderer and would-be rapist later became a monk and was present at Goretti's canonization in 1950. St. Maria Goretti is now the patron saint of chastity, teen girls, and rape victims, among other things, and is often depicted holding a knife.

If I had had the vocabulary at the time, at the tender age of seven, I would have said, "This story is really fucked up." But I didn't know how to say that quite yet, and I instead grappled with my feelings about this story, feelings for which I also lacked an adequate vocabulary. It struck me as very wrong that this thing called virginity, a concept which I did not fully grasp but understood to be good, because it was associated with Mary, the Mother of God, should be prized above all things, including a young girl's life, a young girl who shared my name, thus making my connection to the story all the more personal and urgent. I was also fairly confident that the Jesus I was learning about in school and church would not think it was cool that this teenage girl died in order to preserve this thing called virginity. But now, looking back at this moment, I have the vocabulary to name how this story shaped me. I can put my finger on the maelstrom of emotions that this story provoked, this mixture of confusion, disgust, anger, and fear: that was when I first became a feminist.

But it's only in retrospect that I can identify this pivotal moment. If you had asked me as a teenager what feminism meant (at which point I was regularly grinding my teeth with anxiety rather than pulling them out) I would have told you that being a feminist meant believing that men and women were created equal and should be treated equally. I might have said that feminism was about women having choices, about being empowered to take action. I would have told you that feminism meant that women could be independent and powerful and influential, just like my Mama Teresa. I might have cited a popular bumper sticker that asserts that feminism is the radical notion that women are people, too. In a nutshell, that is perhaps what it is. But if we are to crack the shell, there is a lot more to see than just a nut.

There are multiple theories, both simple and complex, that define what feminism is and what its concerns are. In general, I use the word "feminist" to refer to the academic discipline concerned with exposing and challenging gender inequity and the oppression of women. One definition of feminism tells us:

> Feminism is both the belief that women should be treated equally to men as well as a political movement that works to gain rights and privileges for women. Feminism attempts to explain and eradicate the domination, oppression, and subordination of women. It is a perspective that helps women and men better understand those forces at work in society that create and perpetuate inequality ("Feminism," 2001).

This focus on inequality is also echoed in Crabtree, Sapp, and Licona's (2009) definition of feminism, which notes that feminism is an often contested concept that "encompasses ideas about the importance of women and women's experiences [...] often using misogyny as an organizing principle to explain inequalities and injustices [...]" (p. 1). Thus, a feminist lens is a way of interrogating and problematizing the inequalities that all marginalized people face, not just that of women, and is concerned with issues such as racism, homophobia, and xenophobia.

At age seven, I knew there was a fundamental injustice at the heart of St. Maria Goretti's story. This sense of injustice has been provoked by multiple occasions since reading the story of St. Maria Goretti, growing and intensifying and becoming more sophisticated and less ineffable. It is with a mature woman's lens that I apply feminism to my worldview, but at heart, I am still seven years old, confused, and distressed by what I wordlessly knew to be wrong.

Intuition

Intuition is about gut feelings. That wordless knowledge I had at age seven was intuition. I knew instinctively that valuing female virginity over life itself was wrong. These kinds of gut feelings are typically not valued in academia. Feminism, however, reclaims and values gut feelings. So does this mean that feminism is not valued in academia? It is marginalized, to be sure. I have felt extremely insecure over my writing style in this chapter, which is a definite departure from the more scholarly tone I adopt in later chapters. But I persist in writing this way nonetheless, because my instincts, my gut, my intuition tells me that what I have to say—and the way I'm saying it—has value.

The concept of intuition is certainly a gendered one, and not in ways that portray women as particularly rational. According to Belenky, Clinchy, Goldberger, and Tarule (1984):

> It is likely that the commonly accepted stereotype of women's thinking as emotional, intuitive, and personalized has contributed to the devaluation of women's minds and contributions, particularly in Western technologically oriented cultures, which value rationalism and objectivity. It is generally assumed that intuitive knowledge is more primitive, therefore less valuable, than so-called objective modes of knowing. Thus, it appeared likely to us that traditional educational curricula and pedagogical standards have probably not escaped this bias. (p. 6)

When I do a search for "intuition" in GenderWatch, which provides access to articles in women's and gender studies, I get, among other things, a slew of New Agey articles talking about goddesses, psychic powers, lighting candles, midwifery, casting spells, and reading tarot cards. In a way, these kinds of search results make sense, since GenderWatch contains materials from the sort of unconventional, marginalized, small press feminist literature that concerns such topics. According to GenderWatch, "All the titles featured in the GenderWatch database offer unique, distinctive voices seldom heard in mainstream media. Sometimes outspoken, always informative, the collection represents multiple viewpoints from a wide variety of publications. From scholarly analysis to popular opinion, GenderWatch encompasses more than three decades of gender studies." So while it does contain scholarly literature, the keyword "intuition" turns up articles that are decidedly unscholarly. However, searching "intuition" in Academic Search Premier, a multidisciplinary database, turns up articles in psychology, philosophy, nursing, and other academic fields. Academic Search Premier purports to provide full text articles for almost 4,000 scholarly journals. While you can find newspapers and magazines in Academic Search Premier, you definitely won't find the non-mainstream feminist literature that gets relegated to and ghettoized in GenderWatch.

So why can't I find any serious, academic articles on intuition in women's and gender studies? Or, put differently, why can't I find any patriarchy-approved, androcentric-worldview-having articles on intuition in women's and gender studies? Because isn't that what it means to be "serious" and "academic" and "scholarly"? Not necessarily. If feminism truly values women's ways of knowing, then must it include this other sense of intuition, the kind of intuition that involves candles and spells and psychics? Maybe there's some in between place, between tarot cards and analytic philosophy, which values the inner voice, that quiet way of knowing, that is contrary to the stereotypical, empirical, androcentric way of knowing. Here I'm talking about intuition in the sense of "a rapid form of understanding, knowledge, or meaningful cognition arrived at without the conscious use of reasoning or deliberation" (Rea, 2001, p. 98).

And what does it say about the library profession that non-mainstream feminist literature doesn't belong in a "serious" multidisciplinary article database? It is certainly suggestive that various kinds of feminist literature is not scholarly and is not something to be taken seriously.

Experiential Knowledge

The Personal Narratives Group, a collaborative feminist scholarship effort, (1989) argues that "knowledge, truth, and reality have been constructed as if men's experiences were normative, as if being human meant being male" (p. 3). This androcentric worldview invalidates and erases the woman's point of view. Men traditionally have epistemological privilege. Epistemological privilege means that your way of knowing and method of knowledge production is favored and taken for granted, that your way of knowing is the world's way of knowing, society's way of knowing, that you're in sync, in alignment. This book, for the most part, is an effort to conform to Western ways of knowing, with epistemological privilege. But this book also tries to use feminist technique in its creation and production, thus its privileging of narrative, intuition, and experience. This book wants to resist the epistemological imperative to know things in accordance with the way patriarchy makes things known.

Academic feminism is one way of resisting this imperative. I came to know academic feminism through how I've come to know most things in my life as an insatiable reader: through literature. When I was a sophomore in high school, my English teacher, Mrs. Schuck, assigned us to read poems by Anne Sexton and Sylvia Plath. I remember Plath's poem "Sow" in particular. I was riveted by these poems and had an urgent need to read more, more, more. I went to my high school library and checked out all of the Plath and Sexton books I could find, which I don't think were a whole lot, so I went to the public library to find more books. As I delved into the scholarship on Plath and Sexton, as a mere 15- or 16-year-old, I think I understood about half of what I read, but I knew, intuitively, that feminism was critical to my readings of Plath and Sexton. Plath and Sexton spoke to the inner ache of sexism, among other things, in their beautiful poems, and I knew that their poems were maybe the truest things I'd ever read.

Another early encounter with academic feminism also happened in high school, when my senior year English teacher, Mrs. Clements, had us read *The Awakening* by Kate Chopin and *The Yellow Wallpaper* by Charlotte Perkins Gilman. The tales of women driven mad or driven to suicide by the sexist social mores of the cultures in which they lived made a deep impression upon me. Once again, I turned to the scholarly literature on these works that spoke to me, and I hungrily read the feminist interpretations of these works. Reading this literature and criticism felt like a subversive act in my sheltered Roman Catholic upbringing, and it provided a glimpse of a different way of being and living, a life spent confronting sexism and rebelling against it, a possibility I found tantalizing, and which influenced my decision to eventually be an English major when an undergraduate at Northern Kentucky University.

A critical, pivotal interaction with academic feminism came to me in college, not through a course I was taking, but through a course my friend Erin Kate was taking at a different university. She had recently read Adrienne Rich's "Compulsory Heterosexuality and Lesbian Existence" and urged me to read it, too. She lent me her copy, and I was blown away. I knew of Adrienne Rich through reading her poetry, but this essay was something else altogether. I was not out yet at this point. I had my suspicions about my burgeoning sexuality, but it was all still theoretical at that point. I was still too tethered to my Catholic upbringing to truly confront this theory. But reading this essay concretized this theory into something beyond theory, something I knew to be true, something real. The idea that lesbianism was an expression of feminism struck me as revolutionary and groundbreaking and perfectly logical. Through Erin Kate, I continued reading feminist critical theory, from Helene Cixous to Luce Irigaray to Julia

Kristeva, and while I didn't always understand what they were talking about in my first read, I knew that what they were saying was important and true.

I continued voraciously consuming feminist literature and criticism as I graduated from college and eventually began a graduate program in English at the University of Louisville. As I studied more critical theory and the works of feminist writers like Gertrude Stein and Virginia Woolf, I also met and started dating my first girlfriend. I came out. In this way, academic feminism and lesbian identity are inextricably connected in my mind.

Concluding Thoughts

I have told you a bunch of stories in this first chapter, and perhaps you're wondering what all of this has to do with library instruction. What I'm trying to do here is tell a story about feminism and how I came to know it as a way of foregrounding my later analysis of feminist pedagogy and its connections to library instruction. As I did my research for this book, and as I came to understand how feminist knowledge is created and disseminated and exemplified, I realized that I couldn't talk about feminism without talking about how I came to know it through the life experiences I've just narrated.

My tone will change as this book progresses, and my writing will become more scholarly, but I'm still going to tell stories. I want you, the reader, to think about your own connections to feminism, academic and otherwise, and see me as my Mama Teresa threatening to pull out your tooth. I am tying a string to the doorknob. But you, you can pull out your own tooth and make your own way with Mama Teresa, your first example of feminism, as your guide.*

---

* Opposite page: Maria Teresa and Mama Teresa, Thanksgiving, 1980

2.

Feminist Pedagogy

Why Feminist Pedagogy?

Why does feminist pedagogy matter? Let me begin this chapter telling you some more stories.

A criminal justice professor contacted me to schedule a library instruction session for his first year seminar class. When I asked him what sort of assignment the students had and the topics they would be researching, the professor informed me that they were studying "illegal immigration" and how it was destroying communities, spreading disease, causing crime rates to increase, and all sorts of other blatantly false and xenophobic things. I taught the session, but I talked to students about vocabulary and terminology and how concepts can be described in different ways. "Undocumented workers," for example, was another way of referring to "illegal immigrants." And when I demonstrated how to use the library catalog, searching "immigration and legislation," the first search result that came up was a book called *"They Take Our Jobs!" and 20 Other Myths about Immigration.* Since feminism is not just concerned with sexism, but also racism and xenophobia, I chose to display this myth-busting result as a way of teaching students how to read a bibliographic record.

A student at the reference desk wanted to find articles "proving" that depicting homosexuality positively on television is actually a bad thing, because it is wrong to be a homosexual. I pointed out that I happened to be a homosexual. I was so shocked and emotionally distressed by his blatant homophobia that I didn't have the presence of mind to also point out that the research actually indicates the opposite and that he was going to have a hard time finding articles to "prove" his point. Feminism is also concerned with homophobia, so I saw my coming out to him as a feminist act.

An honors student in a research consultation wanted to investigate who were the best golfers in the history of golf. When I asked him if he already had any particular great golfers in mind, all of the golfers he listed were men. When I pointed out that he was leaving out women in his deliberations, he seemed surprised, and he grudgingly admitted that he supposed "lady golfers" could also be considered in his definition of golfing greatness.

In a faculty senate committee meeting, a male faculty member referred to listserv discussions about gender inequity in faculty service—i.e. women doing a disproportionate amount of service compared to men—as "bitching." I told him that I was offended by his choice of words, especially since it pertained to a discussion of gender issues. He grew defensive, changed his word choice to "fussing," and apologized for using the word "bitching" at an "inopportune" time.

As these personal stories illustrate, feminist pedagogy matters because the higher education system is still tethered to the dominant patriarchal, sexist, racist, and homophobic culture from which it emerged. As Belenky, Clinchy, and Goldberger (1997) note, "Conceptions of knowledge and truth that are accepted and articulated today have been shaped throughout history by the male-dominated majority culture" (p. 5). And as bell hooks (1994) observes, "The politics of domination are often reproduced in the educational setting" (p. 39). Thus, a patriarchal culture produces patriarchal educational systems. The cultural apparatuses that serve to oppress women and perpetuate oppression of marginalized peoples do not disappear once a teacher or a student walks into a classroom.

These stories I'm telling are examples of feminist pedagogy in action, a pedagogy that seeks to bring about social change by raising consciousness about oppression and that values personal experience and testimony as "the fertile ground for the production of liberatory feminist theory" (hooks, 1994, p. 70). In a culture that has historically silenced women's voices and invalidated their lived experiences, feminist pedagogy seeks to reclaim women's experiences, voices, feelings, and ideas in educational settings. Not only is feminist pedagogy concerned with subverting patriarchal subject matter, but it also is concerned with the way any subject matter is taught. Feminist teachers favor active learning techniques. Instead of the teacher serving as the ultimate authority on all knowledge and information, knowledge is collaboratively discussed and created by the students and the teacher together. The students are not passive vessels waiting to be filled by the teacher's wisdom. Lectures are replaced with group discussions with the desks arranged in a circle, and the teacher sitting in the circle. And why would a teacher want to employ feminist teaching strategies? Teachers who care about the souls of students should find ways of teaching that respect student agency, autonomy, and knowledge (hooks, 1994). And when student agency is respected, students are empowered to learn and to bring about social change rather than being passive consumers of knowledge and culture. Feminist teaching strategies propose to do just that, because it is the right thing to do, and in small ways, it can change lives, society, and culture.

Definitions

Defining Pedagogy

Pedagogy is about the theories of teaching. Crabtree, Sapp, and Licona (2009) state that pedagogy "refers to the art, craft, and science of teaching" (p. 1). It is an important field of study, even though it is a term that is often unfamiliar to those involved in teaching (Crabtree, Sapp, & Licona, 2009). And according to *The Social Science Jargon Buster*, "Pedagogy focuses on strategies, techniques, and approaches used to facilitate learning. Critical pedagogy is also interested in learning facilitation, but is primarily concerned with exposing the interests involved in the production and dissemination of knowledge" ("Pedagogy/critical pedagogy", 2007).

While the concept of information literacy in the context of librarianship has been around since the 1970s, "it is only since the beginning of the IL movement in the late 1980s that the potential role of libraries in *facilitating*, rather than just supporting, learning has received any sort of consideration in domains outside of librarianship" (McGuinness, 2011, p. 2). That is, the idea that librarians might be concerned at all about pedagogy is a fairly recent phenomenon. And as the information literacy movement was burgeoning, it was not without its cynics. For example, Foster (1993) asserts that "Information literacy, I would suggest, is largely an exercise in public relations. It is a response to being ignored by the establishment, an effort to deny the ancillary status of librarianship by inventing a social malady with which librarians as 'information professionals' are uniquely qualified to deal" (p. 345). This marginalization and dismissiveness of the concept of information literacy exemplified by Foster has declined as the movement gained more traction in the 1990s and 2000s. Nevertheless, it is still worth noting that it was in this disregarded, almost contemptuous context in which librarians began reshaping their identities as teachers. And while information literacy is now a widely accepted concept, library school education is still lagging behind when it comes to instruction in information literacy pedagogy.

Sproles, Johnson, and Farison (2008), in an analysis of library school required reference course sample syllabi, found that 66 percent of students were introduced to the concept of information literacy. As Sproles, Johnson, and Farison astutely point out, "This was surprising considering the high demand information literacy skills have in entry level academic reference jobs and the applicability of instruction training in many different non-academic library settings" (p. 207). The study also found, however, that courses in information literacy instruction are more common now than they used to be, but that while some ACRL information literacy goals were addressed in these courses, "no classes addressed every proficiency" (p. 207).

These findings are consistent with my own experience in library school. In my reference resources and services course at the School of Information Sciences (SIS) at the University of Pittsburgh, the concept of information literacy was briefly addressed but not in any real depth. SIS did offer a course on information literacy instruction, however, but it was only offered in the summer term, and it did not fit with my schedule. So instead, I developed an independent study, where I read everything I could get my hands on about information literacy. This was the academic preparation I had in library instruction.

Defining Feminist Pedagogy

The previous definition of critical pedagogy is important, because feminist pedagogy is a form of critical pedagogy. Feminist pedagogy is an educational approach informed by a feminist framework. As such, feminist pedagogy is broadly concerned with social justice and sees education as a site for social change and transformation, exposing and ending oppression against women and all other kinds of marginalization: racism, xenophobia, classism, ableism, and so on. Feminist pedagogy is "designed to disrupt the canon of the academy in order to bring about social change," (Bell, Morrow, & Tastsoglou, 1999), and while a good deal of the literature on feminist pedagogy centers on the women's studies classroom, feminist pedagogy has the potential to transform any classroom. Indeed, Crabtree, Sapp, & Licona (2009) note that "Feminist pedagogy is more than teaching about women or teaching feminist perspectives. Feminist teaching is a reexamination and reimagining of what happens in any classroom [...]" (p. 4). Thus, it is not limited disciplinarily by subject matter. Feminist teaching strategies can be employed in any classroom by any teacher seeking to teach in progressive, liberatory ways.

The feminist pedagogical approach in the library classroom is a fairly new concept in the LIS literature. While Broidy (2007) articulates a teaching approach that investigates the relationship between gender and information, Ladenson (2010) is apparently the first to make explicit in the LIS literature the connection between feminist teaching strategies and how they might be used in library instruction. Ladenson describes methods of using feminist active and collaborative learning techniques to enhance and transform the library instruction classroom from a passive, lecture-based environment into an active, engaged, dynamic experience. Thus, bringing feminist pedagogy into the library instruction classroom promises to provide new ideas and directions for library instruction theory and practice.

Context and History

Feminist pedagogy came into being in the historical moment of the women's movement of the 1970s. Providing new approaches to how teaching and learning are conceptualized and enacted, feminist pedagogy connects feminist theory with classroom practice. The first instance of the concept of feminist pedagogy appears in 1981 in a *Radical Teacher* essay by Berenice Fisher, titled, "What is Feminist Pedagogy?" Fisher's work is the foundation upon which much of the literature on feminist pedagogy is built. According to Fisher, feminist pedagogy "is a perspective on teaching which is anti-sexist, and anti-hierarchical, and which stresses women's experience, both the suffering our oppression has caused and the strengths we have developed to resist it" (p. 20). Feminist pedagogy is concerned with incorporating the women's movement into the practice of teaching, and values consciousness-raising and validates women's perspectives as ways of knowing the world (p. 21). While Fisher does not articulate multiple specific teaching strategies, she does identify consciousness-raising as "a clue to the direction in which feminist pedagogy should move" (p. 23). She also provides a theoretical framework in which new teaching practices might be developed. Fisher's contributions to feminist pedagogy extend beyond this 1981 article in *Radical Teacher*; her work has continued into the 21st century literature on feminist pedagogy.

Fisher's work is important, not just because it appears to be the first instance of feminist pedagogy in the literature, but also because it connects feminist pedagogy to the women's movement of the 1970s, one of the contexts from which feminist pedagogy emerged. In the women's movement, which included feminist activism in all realms of a woman's life—the domestic sphere, the arts, music, and so on— education was one arena that also saw activist energy and transformation. The conceptualization of feminist pedagogy was an effort to bring the efforts of the women's movement into higher education. Consciousness-raising about sexism, racism, homophobia, and other forms of oppression was a key component of this stage of feminist activism. Fisher (1981) asserts that feminist pedagogy "represents an important effort to incorporate some of the central features of the women's movement into the work of teaching" (p. 20). Fisher points out that "being a woman in a patriarchal society means being someone whose experiences of the world are systematically discounted as trivial or irrelevant, unless they are related to specifically feminine concerns, or unless they are the experiences of 'exceptional' women" (p. 21). Systems of cultural and societal oppression are frequently replicated and perpetuated in the educational setting. That is, oppression does not occur in a societal or cultural vacuum; its implications and ramifications extend to all environments. Women are not just marginalized in the home, or in the arts, or in politics. They are marginalized everywhere, and educational settings are no different. Bringing the women's movement into the classroom served to extend its conversations and critiques in a setting that could bring about societal and cultural change. Feminist pedagogy seeks to transform sexist and oppressive systems in a way that disrupts replication in the classroom.

Feminist pedagogy translates the consciousness-raising Fisher describes into teaching strategies that seek to inform and enlighten students about societal injustice and how students might bring about social change. This is accomplished through teaching strategies that are either anti-sexist in content, or anti-sexist in method. That is, the actual subject matter of the class might be about sexism, racism, homophobia, and other forms of oppression. For example, the women's studies field is historically one of the first sites of feminist pedagogy due to the topics with which it is concerned, such as women's history and literature, or the study of gender and sexuality or feminist theory. For instance, a women's history class might have students interview women of a certain age group in order to study and learn from their life testimonies and the historical and cultural context of that time (Friedensohn, 1997). Or a women's studies class might require students to read and critique an article in a feminist publication (Scanlon, 1993).

But feminist pedagogy is also about the *way* teachers teach, regardless of the classroom's primary subject matter. As Carillo (2007) notes, "instructors who practice feminist pedagogy in courses that are not within women's studies face specific challenges" (p. 32). These challenges include students not recognizing feminist teaching as actual teaching, because the teacher does not assert ultimate authority, and because the teacher asks more questions than she answers. However, feminist approaches to facilitating student learning are still possible. Giroux (1989) notes that "a feminist classroom must instruct students in a way that makes them attentive to patriarchy as an ideology that is historically and socially constructed as part of an institutional discourse and material force designed to oppress women" (p. 7). Feminist teaching techniques are anti-hierarchal, student-centered, promote community and collaboration, validate experiential knowledge, discourage passivity, and emphasize well-being and self-actualization (hooks, 1994).

Critical pedagogy is a second and interconnected context to which feminist pedagogy can trace its origins. And within the context of critical pedagogy, which seeks to transform society and achieve social justice through education, feminist pedagogy is, in a way, a response to the sexism inherent in early critical pedagogical thought. Paulo Freire's *Pedagogy of the Oppressed* (1970) is a central and influential work in critical pedagogy. Freire's work is formative to the field for his conceptualization of resisting the banking method of teaching, wherein students are empty vessels waiting to be filled with the knowledge of authoritarian teachers. Freire notes:

> It follows logically from the banking notion of conscious-ness that the educator's role is to regulate the way the world 'enters into' the students. The teacher's task is to organize a process which already occurs spontaneously, to 'fill' the stu-dents by making deposits of information which he or she considers to constitute true knowledge (p. 76).

Resisting this banking method helps students develop "criti-cal consciousness," which "result[s] from their intervention in the world as transformers of that world" (p. 73). Banking methods of teaching and learning involve teaching strategies such as lectures, where learners passively take in knowledge and regurgitate it without processing it or contributing their own knowledge or perspective. By contrast, Freirean critical pedagogy involves dialogue between teachers and learners, where students contribute to the production of knowledge, and whereby they come to understand the oppressive systems that are innately part of the dominant culture. Through their coming to consciousness about the dominant culture, learn-ers are equipped to transform this culture and bring about social change.

Freire's *Pedagogy of the Oppressed* is the foundation of several other theorists' works on critical pedagogy, including Peter McLaren, Henry Giroux, bell hooks, and Ira Shor. Shor's work on critical pedagogy, for example, is also central to the field. Building on Freire's work, in *Critical Teaching and Every-day Life*, Shor (1987) notes that "a pedagogy which empowers students to intervene in the making of history is more than a literacy campaign. Critical education prepares students to be their own agents of social change, their own creators of de-mocratic culture" (p. 48). Echoing Freire's concept of critical consciousness, or *conscientização,* Shor envisions a classroom in which student learning leads to activism and engagement with society and culture.

While indispensable to the field of critical pedagogy, Freire's theories are not without their critiques. Freire's work is considered sexist by some theorists, such as bell hooks. hooks (1994) observes "the way he [...] constructs a phallocentric paradigm of liberation—wherein freedom and the experience of patriarchal manhood are always linked as though they are one and the same" (p. 49). That is, Freire's conflation of liberation and masculinity limits the possibilities of liberation for women. But hooks also acknowledges that while Freire's work has some sexist problems, we can still learn from his insights, and that "feminist thinking empowers engagement in a constructive critique of his work" (p. 49). Rather than dismissing Freire's work because of its patriarchal focus and context, the fact that it is concerned with liberation still makes it useful to feminists, even if the work itself is flawed.

Shor's works on critical pedagogy, like that of Freire, also contain evidence of sexism and are subject to feminist critique. In his discussion of sexism in the classroom, he compares the physical violence women experience to that experienced by racial minorities, and in doing so, he diminishes the assaults women have faced, and describes this violence in the past tense, as though it no longer happens on a regular basis:

> Further, minorities have had centuries of violent subordination, in terms of slavery, race riots, police brutality, vigilante attacks, assassinations, and fire bombings; male dominance of women has also been violent, in terms of rape, battering, incest, harassment, and intimidation, but this physical assault on women did not reach the scale it took in race relations (Shor, 1992, p. 230).

His assertion that the violence women face—that is, the sexism women face—is somehow not as significant or frequent than that experienced by racial minorities is both counterfactual and, ironically, sexist. It also obscures the fact that racial minorities also consist of women as well.

Resisting Definition:
Forms of Feminist Pedagogy

The following is a summary of the multiple forms feminist pedagogy can take. I say multiple forms because there isn't one distinct and precise way of defining feminist pedagogy. It can be difficult to pin down because it has so many branches and parts and offshoots. This is reflected in the sense of uncertainty about itself and what it entails that some of the literature on feminist pedagogy displays. Many of the article titles ask questions: "What is feminist pedagogy?" (Fisher, 1981; Shrewsbury, 1987), "Does the use of journals as a form of assessment put into practice principles of feminist pedagogy?" (Clifford, 2002), "Imagination, hope, and the positive face of feminism: Pro/feminist pedagogy in 'post' feminist times?"(Lambert & Parker, 2006), and, in one case, the article tries to pin it down very precisely: "Theory or practice: What exactly is feminist pedagogy?" (Brown, 1992), noting that feminist pedagogy "is still defining itself, largely through a process of questioning long-standing beliefs and practices in education" (p. 52). And as Crawley, Lewis, and Mayberry (2008) observe: "As feminist scholars, we are routinely asked to support the legitimacy of our work by explicitly answering the question: What makes it feminist?" (p. 2). While these many questions seem to indicate a sense of ambiguity about what feminist pedagogy is and what it is concerned with, the recurrent themes explored in the literature from the early 1980s to the present are suggestive more of certainty than of uncertainty.

Frequent topics in the literature include: envisioning the classroom as a collaborative, democratic, transformative site;

consciousness raising about sexism and oppression; and the value of personal testimony and lived experience as valid ways of knowing. While many of the examples from the literature tend to overlap thematically, I will discuss each theme individually in this chapter. Ultimately, there are multiple themes in the literature because feminist pedagogy takes on so many forms and is impossible to encapsulate neatly and definitively.

Gender Injustice, Sexism, and Social Change

Perhaps the most frequently cited characteristic of feminist pedagogy is a concern with gender injustice, sexism, and oppression against women, and how this concern affects what happens in a classroom. Fisher (1981) emphasizes this in her definition of feminist pedagogy, as do Brown (1992), Crabtree et al. (2009), Fisher (2001), Giroux (1989), Gore (1992), Maher (1987), Sandell (1991), Shrewsbury (1987), and Villaverde (2008). Giroux (1989) notes that "a feminist classroom must instruct students in a way that makes them attentive to patriarchy as an ideology that is historically and socially constructed as part of an institutional discourse and material force designed to oppress women" (p. 7). That is, enacting feminism in the classroom should, according to Giroux and others, take as its primary subject matter issues of patriarchal oppression and sexism, and how these things construct what happens in a classroom and what material is taught. A feminist biology or psychology class, for example, might examine the way male bodies are used in scientific studies. A feminist literature class might focus on women writers, and a feminist history class could examine the roles of women in history.

There a number of methods of feminist teaching approaches in the classroom. Consciousness-raising, which has its roots in the early feminist movement, is a key method of

helping students learn about and become aware of sexist society and culture. Freedman (1990) describes consciousness-
raising as "the sharing of personal-experience with others in
order to understand the larger social context for the experience and to transform one's intellectual or political under-
standings of it" (p. 603). This emphasis on raising students'
consciousness about sexism echoes Paulo Freire's (1970)
concept of critical consciousness, or *conscientização*, or "learning to perceive social, political, and economic contradictions,
and to take action against the oppressive elements of reality"
(p. 35). Indeed, feminist pedagogy traces its roots to the liberatory or critical pedagogy developed by Freire and further
extends the theoretical framework to focus more specifically
on issues of sexism, gender injustice, and the oppression of
women, thus reframing his approach to a feminist approach
of understanding the world.

The emphasis on taking action as theorized by Freire is a
critical component of feminist pedagogy theory and practice,
because feminist pedagogy is a form of education to effect
social change (Brown, 1992; Fisher, 1981; Giroux, 1989;
Gore, 1992; Hoffman & Stake, 1998; hooks, 1994, Maher,
1987; Schneidewind, 1987; Shrewsbury, 1987; Villaverde,
2008). Feminist pedagogy seeks to render visible patriarchy
and sexism while also equipping students with the skills to
change the patriarchy and the world. As Crabtree, Sapp, &
Licona (2009) note, "Feminist teaching is a reexamination
and reimagining of what happens in *any* classroom, indeed of
the relationships between teachers, students, education, and
society" (p. 4). This emphasis on the possibility of any classroom as a possible site for feminist teaching strategies means
that feminist pedagogy is not limited to the women's and
gender studies classroom; any classroom, including the library
instruction classroom, is a potential site of feminist teaching.

In my own experience, the library instruction classroom is
indeed a fruitful location that is well-situated for feminist

teaching approaches. I have taught primarily in mid-South classrooms at urban and suburban four-year universities, and I take seriously the responsibility of consciousness-raising in the classroom. Just because my primary objectives in the classroom are information literacy learning outcomes does not mean that I cannot achieve these outcomes through a feminist lens. For instance, I might choose feminist-themed, gender-related, or women-centered examples in database searching demonstrations. When students are researching career planning and career choice, a popular topic among the student body I currently work with, I may choose topics such as "women in engineering," or "women in computer science" to demonstrate how to generate keywords, formulate search queries, conduct a database search, and evaluate search results. Search results will always include articles about the shortage of women in scientific and technical fields, the obstacles women face in these fields, and how sexism limits their growth and professional development. As a result, the students will not only learn and use basic information literacy skills, but they will also find articles that address sexism in these professions. Through a simple teaching strategy, I have, in one small way, raised students' consciousness about sexism. Whether these small steps will bring about social change is unclear, but what I do believe to be true, and what feminist theory does assert, is that consciousness-raising about sexism is an important step toward effecting social change.

Student Voice

Feminist pedagogy is also concerned with the validity of experiential knowledge, or the knowledge produced through the actual lived experience of students, and privileging students' voices over the teacher's voice, which is no longer viewed as the ultimate authority. (Ellsworth, 1992; Clifford, 2002; Fisher, 1981 & 2001; Giroux, 1989; Hoffman & Stake,

1998; Sandell, 1991; Webb, 2004; Villaverde, 2008). Webb, Walker, and Boller (2004) describe group research projects where the teacher valued students' experiential knowledge and what students come into the classroom already knowing. In this example, the student groups "carefully consider[ed] the input of each team member on each point including logical analysis of personal experience" (p. 420). Group members met regularly and every member was expected to speak at each meeting: "thus, we heard each team member's voice at each meeting" (p. 420). Feminist pedagogy values student voices, and as such, feminist teaching strategies seek ways to facilitate this value. Fisher (1981) argues that "being a woman in a patriarchal society means being someone whose experiences of the world are systematically discounted as trivial or irrelevant, unless they related to specifically feminine concerns, or unless they are the experiences of 'exceptional' women" (p. 21). Thus, it is a feminist act to value the voices of students, especially women, and as Bell, Morrow, and Tastsoglou (1999) observe, feminist pedagogy "place[s] a high value on subjective experience as a route to understanding our lives and the lives of others and emphasize[s] the legitimacy of knowledge that arises from socially marginalized positions" (p. 23). As noted earlier, knowledge produced in the male-dominated culture is traditionally privileged as valid, true, and important, so an emphasis on legitimizing other forms of knowledge, especially the knowledge of oppressed classes, is a feminist act.

Shrewsbury (1987) notes that feminist pedagogical "strategies be developed to counteract unequal power arrangements. Such strategies recognize the potentiality for changing traditional unequal relationships" (p. 8), and that "empowering strategies allow students to find their own voices, to discover the power of authenticity" (p. 9). As Belenky, Clinchy, Goldberger, and Tarule (1997) observe, "conceptions of knowledge and truth that are accepted and articulated today have been shaped throughout history by the male-dominated majority culture" (p. 5), and that "nowhere is the pattern of using male experience to define the human experience seen more clearly than in models of intellectual development" (p. 7).

In my own experience, all too often, I have witnessed the way that male students try to dominate class discussion, talk over and interrupt women, restate or reinterpret what women have already said, or simply dismiss outright what women have to say. As a feminist teacher, I can help value female student voices by intervening when male students dominate or interrupt. I can ask male students to remain silent so that female students can speak. In this way, by creating and safe-guarding space for them to speak, I am valuing female stu-dent voices. When I took my very first course in pedagogy as a graduate student in English, our instructors handed out to each of us one piece of Starburst candy. The candy was pink, orange, red, or yellow. Initiating discussion with the group, our instructors specified that only students with yellow can-dies could speak. Then it was orange's turn, then pink, and so on. This ensured that everyone had a chance to speak and prevented any one person from dominating the discussion, including the instructor. This approach can also be employed in the library classroom, as might the "round robin" ap-proach, in which every person in the room is required to say at least one thing, going around in a circle. If someone does not wish to speak, that person must say "pass" before the person next to him or her is permitted to speak. Feminist instruction librarians might employ similar strategies when facilitating discussion in the library instruction classroom.

But valuing women's voices goes beyond simply ensuring that they have a chance to speak in the classroom. It also means valuing what they have to say. It means responding positively when they do speak, and encouraging them when they falter, struggle, or become reticent. Reassurance while a woman speaks, both with verbal cues and with positive body language, can encourage a female learner to move past the self-deprecation that often emerges when she attempts to assert herself or make her opinion known. Moreover, as a confident woman who feels free to speak openly about my ideas, I can model for female learners what a self-assured female voice might look or sound like. Through my example, they can see that it is possible to be an intelligent and confident female learner. I believe that the feminist teacher has a responsibility to model this behavior for female learners.

The phenomenon of library anxiety is also important to consider in terms of feminist pedagogy, library instruction, and communication skills. Mellon's (1986) conceptualization of library anxiety as a barrier to effective library use pays attention to the affective dimension of learning, the area of learning that concerns how learners feel. When learners are anxious about being in the library, they might be less likely to request assistance. And if they do request assistance, their query will be filtered through that anxiety, which will make it difficult for the learner to express what they need and desire. A librarian taking a feminist approach to teaching communication skills can use the library anxiety moment as an opportunity to validate the student's unique voice and approach to the library encounter. That is, reassuring the student through any expressed anxiety, such as "I have not been in the library in years," or "I don't know how to find anything," or "I had a class on this, but I don't remember anything," is a feminist tactic that is both nurturing and affirming.

Collaborative/Cooperative/Democratic/Community

The feminist classroom is designed to be inherently democratic and collaborative, is a place where all voices are valued, and is also a site where students and teachers partner to create a respectful learning community. The collaborative classroom is a collective and pays attention to the ideas and experiences of women (Fisher, 2001). The learning community is participatory and egalitarian, and it serves as a corrective and critique of patriarchal educational beliefs and practices (Hoffmann & Stake, 1998; Brown, 1992). Thwarting the patriarchal hierarchy that perpetuates and reinforces sexism, feminist collaborative community fosters a nurturing environment where all learners—the knowledge and experiences of learners—are valued. Feminist teachers make use of activities that encourage all students to make their voices heard and support teamwork and collaborative problem solving.

One way in which the democratic, collaborative classroom is fostered is through an emphasis on constructive communication. Basic communication skills for expressing feelings, providing helpful feedback, and participating in group processing are strategies for fostering this classroom environment (Schniedewind, 1987). In the nurturing environment favored by feminist approaches to teaching and learning, learners are supported when they express uncertainty and witness models for effective communication through the teacher's example.

At the reference desk and in the library instruction classroom, it has become evident to me that students struggle to communicate their information needs and desires in effective ways. Many times a student will tell me that they need to find a book about something, but when I probe further, it is clear that they just need information in general, and that periodical articles would also suffice for their needs. In other words, to them, the word "book" simply means "information," because they have not yet learned to articulate that information comes in all sorts of formats. This teachable moment that happens in the classroom or at the reference desk is an opportunity to help students hone their information communication skills so they can more efficiently and successfully articulate and fulfill their needs. The reference transaction can thus be considered a feminist act, and reference librarians are engaging in feminist praxis without even realizing it.

It is also apparent, in my experience, that building community through group communication and processing can have an almost magical effect on the classroom. Developing activities that require students to interact with each other and collaboratively conduct a database search and evaluate the search results may sometimes face resistance from students who prefer to work alone, but I make them do it anyway, because I believe that learning out how to communicate in an educational setting helps students learn from each other and about themselves. An activity that requires group decision-making, such as brainstorming keywords and conducting an effective database search together, can change the energy of the classroom from a passive, dull environment to a vital, dynamic one. It can be as simple as asking for student feedback about what topics they would like to address during the library instruction session, or using student suggestions when demonstrating database searching skills, or having students conduct the demonstrations while guided by other students. It truly becomes a learning community during these moments, and it is a feminist approach that helps make that community possible.

Teacher-student relations/authority/empowerment

Feminist pedagogy seeks to transform the teacher/student relationship and disrupt traditional notions of classroom power and authority. Typically, the teacher is perceived to have the ultimate authority in the classroom while students have limited power or agency or none at all. Feminist teaching strategies are anti-hierarchical and student-centered. Shrewsbury (1987) notes that feminist pedagogy "includes a recognition of the power implications of traditional schooling and the limitations of traditional meanings of the concept of power that embody relations of domination" (p. 8). That is, feminist teaching techniques critique and challenge patriarchal power relations that traditionally govern the classroom. This notion is closely related to the feminist pedagogical principle of the democratic, collaborative classroom. In such a classroom, students are expected to be leaders and to make decisions as a group. The teacher shares rather than demands authority and asks more questions than s/he answers. According to Hoffmann & Stake (1998), the feminist teacher fosters a "participatory classroom community that elicits full and open discussion among students and faculty" (p. 81). In the pedagogical strategies described by Webb, Walker, and Bollis (2004), graduate students were taught empirical research methods via "feminist research groups," in which "the teacher refused to voice a topic preference" (p. 416) for their research projects. The teacher also insisted that when the groups encountered problems that they solve them collectively rather than looking to the teacher for guidance or an answer (p. 421).

Feminist pedagogy does not just seek to transform student/teacher relations in general, but seeks to empower female learners in particular. As Bignell (1996) observes, feminist pedagogy "implies a restructuring of the power relationships in the classroom to favor women and is specifically concerned with empowering female students" (p. 316). Crabtree, Sapp, and Licona (2009) echo this concern with female students, noting that attentiveness to a student's intellectual and personal growth should include "a special care for female students, inside and outside the classroom, and a commitment to advancing and improving the educational experiences, professional opportunities, and daily lives of women" (p. 5).

Ethics of Care

Finally, an important aspect of teacher/student relations concerns an ethic of care. As Crabtree, Sapp, and Licona (2009) note, "feminist teachers demonstrate sincere concern for their students as people and as learners [...]" (p. 4-5). hooks (1994) also references the ethic of care: "To teach in a manner that respects and cares for the souls of our students is essential if we are to provide the necessary conditions where learning can most deeply and intimately begin" (p. 13). The teacher/student relationship, therefore, must take into account the affective dimension of learning, how learners feel about their learning experiences, and how the learning environment influences affect. In my own classroom experience, it is evident to me that students respond well to caring. Just like any other vulnerable human being, they want to be the subject of care. They want to be cared about and cared for. And what makes care feminist is that it sees students as whole human beings, not vessels to be filled with information and knowledge. It sees learners as people with thoughts and feelings that they bring into the classroom, and which, in turn, affect how they learn. Teachers can easily express this care verbally, as well as through his or her actions, by paying special attention to female learners and committing to improving the lives of women (Crabtree, Sapp, & Licona, 2009). Taking the time to listen to students, to honor their voices, to rely on them for examples, and to encourage them to listen to each other all exemplify the ethic of care.

Noddings's (1988) conception of the ethic of caring in the classroom serves as a foundation for much of critical thought about caring. Noddings observes the gendered nature of caring: "As an ethical orientation, caring has often been characterized as feminine because it seems to arise more naturally out of woman's experience than man's" (p. 218). Feminism is, in part, concerned with elevating qualities associated with women and being female, even if not all women share those qualities, so associating the ethic of care with feminist pedagogy makes sense. Noddings notes, however, that when the ethical orientation of caring is reflected upon more fully, it turns out to be what Noddings refers to as "relational ethics" (p. 218), which, presumably, de-genders the ethical orientation of caring. What does this mean for the field of education?

While Noddings focuses on childhood education, Thayer-Bacon and Bacon (1996) describe a model of caring professors in the higher education classroom. According to Thayer-Bacon and Bacon, a caring teacher is personal, takes the time to get to know students, treats students as valued participants and collaborators in the learning environment, helps students learn to believe in themselves, is affirming and nurturing, fosters a safe and kind learning environment, and develops a respectful and trusting relationship with students. This useful theoretical model conceived by Thayer-Bacon and Bacon provides specific characteristics for the caring teacher, a framework that can be borrowed by feminist pedagogy for library instruction.

Another theoretical model of significance regarding the ethic of care comes from a womanist school of thought. As a white cisgender lesbian feminist with privilege, I do not and cannot profess to be a womanist, but I do acknowledge that I have much to learn from womanism, or African American feminism, and it is with great respect that I listen to what womanists have to say.[2] The term womanism originates with Alice Walker in her 1983 text *In Search of Our Mother's Gardens: Womanist Prose,* where she defines womanist as, among other things, "A black feminist or feminist of color" (p. xi), as well as "Responsible. In charge. *Serious,*" (p. xi), and "A woman

---

[2] The womanist approach resonates with me, but definitionally, I cannot take on the identity of womanism, since I am not a woman of color.

who loves other women, sexually and/or nonsexually [...] Committed to survival and wholeness of entire people, male *and* female" (p. xi).

This emphasis on the "survival and wholeness of entire people" is evident in Beauboeuf-Lafontant's 2002 article, which examines the pedagogy of exemplary African American female teachers and articulates what constitutes a womanist pedagogy: "Womanist teachers see racism and other systemic injustices as simultaneously social *and* educational problems. Consequently, they demonstrate a keen awareness of their power and responsibility as adults to contest the societal stereotypes imposed on children" (p. 77). This is an essential, critical point that is worth exploring further. Feminist pedagogy argues that what happens in the world, such as racism, classism, sexism, and other forms of oppression, is mirrored in the classroom. The classroom is not a neutral place; it is inextricably linked to the culture it lives in. This assertion is similarly echoed by Bass (2012), who describes the ethic of care displayed by Black feminist teachers, noting that their own personal experiences predispose them to a form of caring instruction: "In many ways, this genuine form of caring is provided by adults and educators who themselves have suffered from acts of discrimination and oppression and are sensitive to social injustice because of their own personal experiences" (p. 74). Thus, womanism's concern with education as a platform for social justice and change provides a pathway for feminist pedagogy for library instruction to conceive of a new instructional praxis.

Classroom Limitations of Feminist Pedagogy

Feminist pedagogy, while viewed as positive and liberatory by many teachers, may not always be welcomed by students. As Carillo (2007) describes, students sometimes resist the "guide by the side" model of teaching, which involved favoring student input and an absence of lecturing or assertion of authority: "because I did not take on the authoritative role that my students expected, they rejected my teaching practices" (p. 32). Indeed, hooks (1994) notes that "the urge to experiment with pedagogical practices may not be welcomed by students who often expect us to teach in the manner they are accustomed to" (pp. 142-143). Bell, Morrow, and Tastsoglou (1999) observe that students do not always welcome progressive pedagogy, and "instead, they have often resorted to various resistance strategies, ranging from refusal to comply with course requirements to more subtle expressions that appear to undermine our pedagogical efforts" (p. 25). Such pedagogical efforts include feminist and anti-racist course materials, discussions of affirmative action, and a "foreign-accented female instructor" (p. 28), all of which met with resistance and protest, especially from male students. The feminist emphasis on experiential knowledge also met with resistance, but in a way that backfired. The teaching strategies described by Bell, Morrow, and Tastsoglou encouraged students to place personal knowledge and experience within a feminist theoretical context, and students resisted this, instead valuing personal experience to the exclusion of other perspectives (p. 32). Student resistance to the transformation of student/teacher relations is one of the reasons why, as Carillo (2007) notes, "feminist authority thus remains a problematic issue for theories of feminist pedagogy" (p. 34). Students may not respect or listen to teachers who do not act or look how they expect teachers to act or look: male, white, authoritative, assertive, and in-charge.

The question of feminism and authority is an interesting one, because it is true, in my own experience, that sometimes students do resist having to take responsibility for their own learning. They might resist, mock, undermine, or flat-out refuse to participate in activities that are active, student-centered, and developed in the spirit of "guide on the side" versus "sage on the stage." Some students would prefer that I lecture to them about library skills instead of making them work and participate and engage and discuss what the library is all about and why it matters. Some students at the reference desk would just prefer that I give them the needed call number rather than turning the computer screen to them to demonstrate exactly how I found the call number. It often feels easier to give the students what they want and to maintain the traditional, passive, bibliographic instruction model rather than try to create a more dynamic classroom that encourages student participation and values student input. But just because it is easier does not mean that it is the most effective technique for producing and facilitating student learning.

Critiques of Feminist Pedagogy

Student resistance to feminist pedagogy is one way of illustrating its limitations. Critics of feminist pedagogy offer additional shortcomings. Gore (1992) offers a critique of feminist pedagogical notions of empowerment: "Critical feminist pedagogy discourses frequently perpetuate a simplistic dichotomy between empowerment and oppression through a level of abstraction which mystifies the meanings ascribed to either term (empowerment or oppression)" (p. 59). Ellsworth (1992) echoes this critique, arguing that "strategies such as student empowerment and dialogue give the illusion of equality while in fact leaving the authoritarian nature of the teacher/student relationship intact" (p. 98). So while transforming teacher/student relations remains an important component of feminist pedagogy, it is imperative to pay attention to these critiques of the authority that feminist pedagogy seeks to challenge, disrupt, or transform. Gore and Ellsworth usefully identify ways in which feminist techniques, instead of liberating, might reproduce oppression and domination. A feminist teacher should take care to examine his or her approach to decentering classroom authority in order to make certain that the techniques do not, in Gore's words, "serve as instruments of domination despite the intentions of their creators" (p. 54). That is, the ways in which power and authority are conceptualized in feminist pedagogy are often overly simplistic and obscure the actual meanings and implications of the terms, which, in turn, ultimately reinforces the hierarchy it seeks to abolish. Others argue that it is important to destabilize authority and embrace student empowerment "while still retaining sufficient control in the classroom to evaluate and grade effectively, as well as to maintain respect and student responsibility" (Torrens & Riley, 2004, p. 69).

And the feminist ethic of care is itself subject to feminist critique. Villaverde (2008) notes that the ethic of care tends to reinforce stereotypes of women as nurturers while still arguing that "Care is essential in creating sustainable social spaces for learning, but care must be politicized and held accountable to the interrelationship of overlapping modes of oppression" (p. 127). That is, care should not be confused with paternalism or condescension, which are typically patriarchal approaches to care in the classroom. And despite her apparent effort to distance the ethic of care from gender, Noddings (1988) compares caring teachers to maternal caring: "Teachers, like mothers, want to produce acceptable persons—persons who will support worthy institutions, live compassionately, work productively but not obsessively, care for older and younger generations, be admired, trusted and respected" (p. 221). This is a curious comparison that seems to erase the possibilities of mothers who are not caring or engaged with their children, or fails to consider that fathers, or any parental figure, for that matter, can have these same sentiments. Despite these problems, however, Noddings does provide us with a starting point for considering the ethic of care in the context of teaching.

What Feminist Pedagogy Looks Like in the Library Classroom

So what does feminist teaching look like in the classroom? Belenky et al. (1997) describe the teacher as midwife, which is, by definition, the opposite of banking method teaching, which views students as passive vessels waiting to be filled with the teacher's wisdom and knowledge: "While bankers deposit knowledge in the learner's head, the midwives draw it out. They assist the students in giving birth to their own ideas, in making their own tacit knowledge explicit and elaborating it" (p. 217). Thus, the feminist approach to teaching and learning rejects the banking model favored by the patriarchal paradigm of education, described by Freire (1970) and others. Specific feminist teaching strategies that encourage students to identify and articulate their own ideas are outlined briefly below, and these will be examined in closer detail in Chapter 3.

The feminist teacher:	The feminist instruction librarian:
Makes use of the seminar discussion-based format, which fosters active participation and values student voices (Broidy, 2007; Chow et al., 2003).	Promotes active participation when discussing possible research topics, database searching strategies, or other information literacy learning activities.
Is characterized by the absence of lecturing and assertion of authority. Instead, the teacher asks for student input (Carillo, 2007).	Relies on student input for database demonstration, keyword brainstorming, and search query formation.
Emphasizes hands-on or interactive learning, field trips, service or community learning (Chow et al., 2003).	Employs hands-on learning activities that require students to engage with library research tools.
Facilitates cooperation, class participation, group work;	Makes use of group work or partner work for information

builds community; involves students in decision making; elicits personal responses to material (Duncan & Stasio, 2001).	searching or evaluation. Develops learning activities that solicit and validate students' experiential knowledge.
Employs consciousness-raising (Fisher, 1981).	Raises awareness of sexism and other forms of oppression through library research content and examples (e.g. using "women in engineering" for a search topic in a career research class.)
Is attentive to language as a way of constructing reality and knowledge; acknowledges central role of language in teaching, learning, and theory formation (Giroux, 1989).	Takes care to explain how keywords and/or subject terms often fail to take into account or adequately describe marginalized people or topics. Demonstrates how to rephrase search language in order to retrieve satisfactory results.
Uses egalitarian classroom practices, encourages student development of personal strengths, and fosters social relations that challenge patriarchy (Giroux, 1989).	Makes use of learning activities that validate learners' talents and strengths and invite students to share or demonstrate skills for class. Fosters an anti-hierarchical classroom environment where student input is sought, utilized, and valued.
Fosters an environment in which all individuals work together to achieve goals collectively (Hayes, 1989).	Collaboratively develops goals and learning outcomes for library session with students. Invites suggestions from students on how to achieve goals.
Encourages students to define key terms for class discussion (Maher, 1985)	Seeks student input on keyword brainstorming. Encourages students to help set the agenda for learning activities and goals for the session.

Supports students in achieving mastery on their own or in collaborative group exercises (Parry, 1996).	Develops learning activities that allow students to improve and hone library research skills individually or with partners/groups.
Makes use of reflective personal journals (Parry, 1996).	Employs learning activities or assessment instruments that promote student reflection on learning and research process and facilitate metacognition.
Employs networked computerized classrooms, which can shift power relationships and promote active learning (Parry, 1996).	Uses computer classroom in a way that empowers individual learners and promotes hands-on kinesthetic learning.
Focuses on interaction, such as impromptu speaking, group exercises, ice-breakers, keeping people meeting new people, changing physical environment (Torrens & Riley, 2004).	Keeps the classroom interesting and lively by encouraging students to speak, work in groups, and move around the classroom.
Makes use of think/pair/share, team work and team reports, and group problem-solving (Webb et al., 2004)	Develops learning activities that require students to work individually, then share with a partner, and then share with the group. Provides problem-based research scenarios for students to solve together.

Conclusion

Feminist pedagogy is an approach to teaching and learning that seeks to transform the lives of learners and the society in which the classroom exists. Tracing its origins from the women's movement and the critical pedagogy movement, feminist pedagogy teaches learners about sexism explicitly as a topic, or implicitly through anti-sexist, anti-hierarchical teaching strategies. Feminist teachers foster a holistic, nurturing environment that equips students to change themselves and change the world.

As noted in the introduction, there is not, as of this writing, a book-length work or periodical article in the literature that explores the connections between library instruction and feminist pedagogy. Save for a single article in a book that I co-edited (Ladenson, 2010), all of the literature on feminist pedagogy is about classroom realms other than the library. Women's studies is the predominant field in which feminist pedagogy is investigated, which makes sense, given the subject matters with which women's and gender studies is concerned.

The time is right, right now, to bring feminist pedagogy into conversation with library instruction. Librarians are already employing active, learner-centered, anti-hierarchical teaching strategies without explicitly identifying these techniques as feminist. Let's see what we are already doing, and what we could be doing, and fully understand the feminist implications of our pedagogical strategies.

3.

Feminist Teaching in the
Library Instruction Classroom

As I lay sleepless in the narrow bed of my Champlain College dorm room, suffering from stress-induced insomnia and an airplane-germs-cold, I wept silently as I thought anxiously about my impending final project—an instruction program improvement action plan—for the ACRL Immersion Program. I had been at Immersion all week, learning how to be an ACRL-approved teacher. Emotionally exhausted by long days of learning and social interaction and group activities with a cohort of other library instruction coordinators—including listening to lectures from the Immersion faculty, being asked to express my feelings via Play-Doh, endless PowerPoint presentations about learning outcomes and active learning and pedagogy (some of which were in Comic Sans font), a surreal social outing to the Trapp Family Lodge where hundreds of instruction librarians sang "How Do You Solve a Problem Like Maria" in unison, and an ice cream social where I hastily made a sundae and then just as hastily scurried back to my dorm room, paralyzed by social anxiety—this overwhelmed introvert was Having Some Feelings. The affective dimension of learning is no joke. I wondered if this was how my students felt when I overwhelmed them with information during a library instruction session. As I eventually drifted off into a fitful, sniffly sleep, I was struck with a new sense of empathy for my students and their feelings about learning. I hope that the ghost of Paulo Freire will forgive me for thinking of this moment as my Immersion *conscientização*, or coming to critical consciousness. It was a moment in my journey as a feminist teacher that underscored for me the central importance of care and compassion for my students.

But my journey as a feminist teacher is not always quite so dramatic and emotional. Care and compassion are important, yes, but being a feminist teacher can also be fun and energizing. One of my favorite library instruction moments in recent memory involved a first year seminar American history class, Martha Washington, and a time machine. In a last minute flash of creative energy an hour before my class was to begin, I ditched my boring lesson plan and decided to put Lady Washington in the time machine and have her arrive in my library instruction classroom, just to see what would happen. Of course, at this late hour, it was too late to hire a Martha Washington impersonator or construct a time machine, so this was an imaginary time machine and an imaginary Lady Washington and the whole enterprise required my students to join me in my flight of fancy. After the imaginary Lady Washington arrived, I asked my students to explain to her how libraries and information have changed since her time. This activity actually sparked discussion—that exciting, elusive thing that all librarian instructors yearn for—and then we moved from discussion to practice searching article databases. I consider it one of my most successful brainstorms. The students learned something, the teaching faculty member was happy, and I was happy. Win, win, win. And, although the students didn't fully realize it, I had sneaked some feminist pedagogy in there, too.

This chapter will position current library instruction practice, both overt and implicit, in the framework of feminist pedagogy. In particular, it will examine feminist approaches to information literacy learning outcomes and teaching strategies. It will also realistically highlight the challenges of such practices within the constraints most library instructors face, while still having hope in its possibility. bell hooks (1994) invites us to teach in a way that "cares and respects for the souls of students," even if the situation does not allow for the "full emergence of a relationship based on mutual recognition" (p. 13). This is particularly relevant to the limits of time and space faced by instruction librarians, who have much to accomplish in a short time period, and who labor under the pressures of ACRL standards and proficiencies and the occasional indifferent faculty member.

As I've been writing this book, I've found myself challenged by a number of critical, central questions. Why isn't it enough to just be a feminist? Why do I have to be a feminist teacher? My answer to this is that the personal is indeed political. I am a feminist; therefore I am a feminist teacher. Incorporating feminist practice and critique into teaching practice is a way of making a difference. As a feminist teacher librarian, I want students to not just have information literacy skills. I want them to be lifelong critical thinkers and learners. The project of information literacy is concerned with this same notion of lifelong learning. So is feminist pedagogy. Feminist instruction librarians want critical thinkers to then become critical actors.

Feminism already is, in a way, informing our teaching practices, in that library instruction favors active learning, a nurturing environment, and learner-centered pedagogy. We are already doing this. Why make the politics more explicit? Because this is how social change happens. This is how lives are transformed, the lives of both teacher and learner. Critical actors take the knowledge they have learned in the feminist classroom and translate it into everyday life and society and culture. They are more aware of forms of oppression and act to end them. They are aware of the power of knowledge and language to influence society and culture and they ask critical questions about where information comes from, about who decides what is knowledge and truth, thus illuminating the structures that create and perpetuate information production and dissemination.

This is what makes feminist pedagogy different from learner-centered teaching: critical thinkers become critical actors. While learner-centered approaches to teaching are concerned with what the learner ends up learning, the feminist approach cares about what the learner does with the knowledge gained in and outside the classroom.

The Learning Paradigm and the Shift from BI to IL

In order to understand how feminist pedagogy can make an impact on library instruction, it is important to have a fuller understanding of the field of library instruction, its origins, its purpose, and its models. Today, library instruction programs at institutions of higher education are typically based on the principle of teaching information literacy skills, as defined by the Association of College and Research Libraries. In short, information literacy "is the set of skills needed to find, retrieve, analyze, and use information" (ACRL, 2000). The library profession has been the primary proponent of the notion of information literacy, and in the past decade, the teaching approach of academic library instruction programs has shifted from bibliographic instruction to information literacy instruction. I characterize bibliographic instruction (BI) as a more passive, tools-based approach that focuses on how to use a particular library resource without paying much attention to critical thinking or transferable skills. A BI session might take place in a non-networked classroom, with the instructor at the only computer, pointing and clicking through the library catalog or article database. Or the librarian instructor might roll in a cart full of print reference books to hold aloft and page through in front of the class. In an information literacy classroom, active learning is encouraged, and learning takes place in a networked classroom where each student has a computer. Rather than relying heavily on passive demonstration, which is more typical of BI, an information literacy instruction session provides space for students to learn in a collaborative, hands-on manner. And rather than focusing on how to use a particular tool, the focus is on critical thinking skills and how they can be deployed across any library platform, no matter what the interface.

In his discussion of BI versus information literacy instruction, Gibson (2008) notes that:

> Bibliographic instruction continues to possess a valuable but limited role in helping sustain students' ability to cope with the confusing array of resources in the landscape before them—but it is not well-suited to the future because it focuses on formulaic, often linear, two-dimensional strategies for finding and evaluating information in a landscape where students are often wondering "Where am I?" (p. 13).

In contrast, Gibson characterizes the information literacy model as "a programmatic, curriculum-integrated, and pervasive and sustained placement of information and research skills throughout the curriculum" (p. 12). In this model, information literacy is a general education student learning outcome, and thus it has priority as something with institutional value. It is integrated throughout the curriculum through credit-bearing courses, or through tiered and targeted library instruction programs that provide one-shot library instruction sessions for students at multiple levels of their college career. This might include the first year seminar level, the entering the major/intermediate level, and the senior seminar/capstone level.

This paradigm shift from bibliographic instruction to information literacy instruction is consistent with the shift from instruction models to learning models in higher education. This shift that privileges learning over teaching, in turn, makes the field more open to feminist pedagogical critiques and interpretations. The Instruction vs. Learning Paradigms, as theorized by Barr and Tagg (1995), are useful frameworks for tracing this transition. As Barr and Tagg describe, the traditional model of higher education has centered on instruction. In this teacher-focused Instruction Paradigm, "colleges have created complex structures to provide for the activity of teaching conceived primarily as delivering 50-minute lectures" (para. 2). The Instruction Paradigm is similar to Freire's concept of banking model, which favors the instructor's knowledge over the student's learning. However, in the Learning Paradigm, "our mission is not instruction but rather that of producing learning with every student by whatever means work best" (para. 3). That is, what matters is that the student learns. Whatever pedagogical tactics the instructor chooses is not of utmost importance as long as learning happens. This is more in line with Freire's critical pedagogy model. When bringing the Barr and Tagg framework into conversation with library instruction, it is evident that the bibliographic instruction model is consistent with the Instruction Paradigm, while information literacy instruction is characteristic of the Learning Paradigm, which focuses primarily on the student learning experience.

This shift from bibliographic instruction/Instruction Paradigm to information literacy/Learning Paradigm is also, in a way, feminist: as in the Learning Paradigm, the traditional, patriarchal structures of education are dismantled and replaced with egalitarian learner/learning centered structures. Like patriarchy, the Instruction Paradigm is a mostly invisible cluster of unexamined assumptions:

> Its incoherencies and deficiencies appear as inherent qualities of the world. If we come to see the Instruction Para-

digm as a product of our own assumptions and not a force of nature, then we can change it. Only as you begin to experiment with the new language will you realize just how entrenched and invisible the old paradigm is. But as you and your colleagues begin to speak the new language, you will then also begin to think and act out of the new paradigm (Barr & Tagg, 1995, p. 25)

Therefore, the educational system, rooted in the patriarchal culture from which it emerged, can be transformed through experimentation with student-centered learning, as Barr and Tagg assert, and through feminist approaches to teaching, which primarily seek to destabilize traditional, hierarchical, and sexist models of teaching and learning. This has exciting and potentially transformative implications for library instruction.

Learning Outcomes and the Cult(ure) of ACRL

Learning outcomes are at the root of the Learning Paradigm and information literacy instruction. This centrality of learning outcomes is also a concern that feminist pedagogy shares. Student learning outcomes describe what a student will be able to do as a result of the learning experience and what impact that learning will have on that behavior. As described by Gilchrist and Zald (2008), "Learning outcomes are specific statements that express our hopes for our students' learning" (p. 168). In other words, learning outcomes are how we articulate how we want our students to perform as a consequence of the teaching and learning encounter. I like the Gilchrist and Zald definition of learning outcomes for its affect and optimism. Unfortunately, this optimism is in opposition to how learning outcomes are often deployed. Given that they are valued by cultures of power such as institutions or accrediting bodies, learning outcomes sometimes appear to reinforce the traditional, hierarchical, and sexist models of higher education. However, learning outcomes can be viewed as a product of the shift from the learner-centered Instruction Paradigm to the Learning Paradigm, and this is indicative of their potential for feminist critique and interpretation.

The learner-centered nature of learning outcomes give them great feminist potential. Rather than focusing on reproducing the dominant educational paradigm, or depositing knowledge in student's heads, the feminist approach to teaching and learning seeks to transform student/teacher relationships as a way of raising awareness of sexism in higher education and in the culture at large and bringing about social change. Focusing on the student's voice and the validity of his or her experiential knowledge, feminist teachers value student learning and experience. This student-learning focus is the underlying principle of learning outcomes, thus making learning outcomes a powerful tool for feminist instructional design and assessment. This student learning focus is something that instruction librarians already value, even if they do not explicitly acknowledge it as feminist.

Using learning outcomes as a starting point for library instruction instructional design and assessment is a method espoused by most library instruction theorists and practitioners, and I believe that it is an approach that makes sense for feminist instruction librarians as well, because feminist instructional design requires that students are at the center. Gilchrist and Zald's model is particularly useful for instruction librarians seeking a structure for planning instruction sessions:

1.	Outcome:	What do you want the student to be able to do?
2.	Information Literacy Curriculum:	What does the student need to know in order to do this well?
3.	Pedagogy:	What type of instruction will best enable the learning?

4. Assessment:	How will the student demonstrate the learning?
5. Criteria for Evaluation:	How will I know the student has done this well?

Table 1: Gilchrist & Zald, 2008, p. 168

This coherent and concise structure helps provide a useful template for instruction session design. While the process of instruction session planning is not as always linear as these steps describe, each component plays an important part in designing a high quality instruction session rooted in student learning and assessment (Gilchrist & Zald, 2008, p. 168).

This useful model advances feminist teaching principles. As noted in Chapter 1, the feminist approach to teaching is more akin to midwifery rather than banking: "While bankers deposit knowledge in the learner's head, the midwives draw it out. They assist the students in giving birth to their own ideas, in making their own tacit knowledge explicit and elaborating it" (Belenky et al., 1997, p. 217). I argue that the Gilchrist & Zald model is consistent with the feminist pedagogical framework in that it is flexible, student-centered, and focused on drawing out, or giving birth to, student knowledge, skills, abilities, and experiences. The Gilchrist & Zald model is also feminist in that it is conducive to active learning and rejects the lecturing "sage on the stage" patriarchal mode of instruction.

I am focusing on the Gilchrist and Zald model here because it is a model that resonates with me; it is a clear and concise method of conceptualizing, planning, teaching, and assessing a library instruction session. In five steps, it outlines exactly what a librarian needs to do in order to be effective, and it provides a helpful anchor and framework for a librarian who wants a defined structure to govern her teaching practices. It is not the only model, of course, that librarian instructors can follow. Char Booth's USER method (2011), for example, is another useful structure for organizing, delivering, and assessing library instruction. Maintaining a critical consciousness about instructional design and delivery helps a feminist teacher resist the easy slide back into the banking model of teaching.

But learning outcomes aren't necessarily a Band-Aid solution to the problem of the banking method. For example, I learned about Gilchrist & Zald's learning-outcomes-centric model at ACRL's Institute of Information Literacy Immersion Program, which teaches hundreds of academic instruction librarians a year how to think about and approach library instruction and instruction programs. Immersion, and the librarians it churns out, is the product of the dominant culture of power if there ever was one. So while the potential exists for learning outcomes and instructional design to be feminist, how these things are deployed determines how nurturing and learner-centered they really are. Without a reflective, student-centric, compassionate approach, learning outcomes can be used as banking method tools.

One perspective may aver that Immersion is a training ground and boot camp for shaping instruction librarians into an ACRL-approved mold, and following the Gilchrist & Zald model in lockstep, without a feminist, process-oriented mindset, is one way of perpetuating that mold. A mold is a very uncompromising, unyielding object, one that enforces conformity and rigidity. I felt this inflexibility keenly on my last day of Immersion, when, feeling battered and exhausted and kind of like I'd been indoctrinated into a cult, I was asked to fill out lengthy and complex evaluation forms about my experience there. I was stunned to realize that we were only given a short amount of time to fill out the forms. I felt rushed and pressured and shortchanged. I really needed time to digest and reflect in order to give them the feedback I felt the program warranted. But the way they conducted their assessment did not allow for much time to reflect. The irony is that Immersion teaches that assessment and reflection are critical components of any teaching and learning endeavor, but in practice, it wasn't exactly creating space for successful and effective assessment. There was no room in its packed schedule to allow more time for reflection and feedback.

While I am critical of ACRL Immersion's assessment practices, the experience was for the most part helpful. I learned a lot, and I still use some of the ideas and principles in my daily practice. I structure my library instruction sessions using the format they taught us at Immersion. The information they taught us about change management and organizational development was invaluable to me as the coordinator of an instruction program. The friendships I made there last to this day. I still consult my Immersion binder to reread articles I was assigned while I was there. So there is plenty that I got out of it. But there was plenty that I did not like.

ACRL's Immersion is a mindset that is open to critique. It is a dominant culture paradigm that can be subverted for feminist purposes. Critical pedagogy seeks to not just subvert the dominant paradigm, but to reshape it and transform it into something life-altering. Feminism can do just that for ACRL standards and the ACRL approach to library instruction and the ACRL boot camp that is Immersion. If I could go back in time and redo my comments on those hastily-completed evaluation forms, I would recommend that critical pedagogy be a required part of the Immersion curriculum, along with discussions about the political and social realities of information literacy. And, of course, I would suggest that they strengthen their feedback loop. And while the program itself did not seem that open to critique, I still have things to say about what didn't work for me, and what I think that says about ACRL as an organization.

In a sense, I think ACRL's Immersion Program may represent some of the most frustrating aspects of ACRL as an organization and the ideas it promulgates. Namely, the idea that information literacy is some neutral, apolitical concept that exists outside of the culture and paradigm that produced it is problematic to me. Of *course* information literacy is and should be politicized. So should the classroom, the library, and its institution. The racism, sexism, homophobia and other forms of oppression that are perpetuated by the dominant culture do not disappear once we walk into a library classroom. In fact, those oppressions are replicated in the classroom.

So why doesn't ACRL acknowledge this fact in its Standards for Information Literacy or in its Immersion Program? Why does it seem to ignore or erase the very real politics that are alive in the classroom? Standard Five makes gestures toward understanding the social issues surrounding information, but its performance indicators seem to focus on issues like censorship, copyright, security, and legal issues. These performance indicators appear to completely ignore the "social issues" that are asserted to be relevant in the language of Standard Five: "The information literate student understands many of the economic, legal, and social issues surrounding the use of information and accesses and uses information ethically and legally" (ACRL). The social issues surrounding the use of information include things such as the ways in which sexism affects the creation and dissemination of knowledge and how women's ways of knowing are marginalized and invalidated. What if we incorporated these issues into our instructional practices? What would this look like? It would look like feminist pedagogy. Thus, Standard Five appears to hold the most promise for feminist teaching practices in the library instruction classroom and it can be employed to justify feminist teaching practices in the classroom.

What does feminist library instruction look like?

As outlined in the table in the previous chapter, feminist library instruction can take many forms. Using the Gilchrist & Zald model for instruction design and assessment, the following scenarios outline what a feminist library instruction session might look like. In any one library instruction, especially a one-shot session where the librarian may never see those students again, it is important to be selective about which learning outcomes to focus on, because time does not permit an exhaustive approach. My general approach is to attempt to choose one outcome from three of the five areas addressed by ACRL Standards One (Identify), Two (Access), Three (Evaluate), Four (Use), and Five (Ethics). Contexts and lesson plans are available in Appendix A and sample worksheets follow in Appendix B. Assessment techniques are identified in these lesson plans, but feminist approaches to assessment will be explored more fully in the next chapter.

Challenges of feminist library instruction

Feminist library instruction matters, because it equips students with the skills and knowledge to navigate and transform the dominant culture of knowledge production. Instruction librarians who care about their students and want to teach in ways that liberate and validate students and their lived experiences and voices will find feminist approaches to library instruction a worthwhile endeavor. While often touted as the bastion of intellectual freedom, the academic library cannot be separated from the institutional culture in which it lives. While paradigm shifts in higher education are more supportive of feminist pedagogy than older, more traditional models might have been, higher education is still contextualized in the racist, sexist, homophobic, and xenophobic structures that govern our culture. So, too, is the culture of academic librarianship, which is held in thrall to the apolitical dictates of ACRL standards.

Clifford (2002) asks an interesting question: whether a feminist ideological approach to teaching and learning should take precedence over other agendas. Translated into our context, I might ask: which matters more: that students learn about information literacy, or that they are made more aware of sexism and oppression and are equipped to change society and the world? Ultimately, however, I don't think this is a fair or necessary question or an either/or binary proposition. I believe that library instruction can do both: teach about information literacy and teach about feminism. Institutionally, the priority is information literacy, but there can be room within institutional agendas for political activism. And, in the end, education is always political; it does not take place in a neutral vacuum.

Like anything new and different, resistance to change makes feminist teaching approaches a challenge in the library instruction classroom. Reluctance to disrupt the status quo and codes of the dominant culture of higher education and library instruction theory and practice also make it difficult to enact liberatory, progressive teaching practices. Instructors who hold these values often find themselves in opposition to the higher education culture, as Eisenhower and Smith (2010) observe: "a rhetoric of critical pedagogy put into play in the context of this particular learning organization [...] positions us as educators in opposition to organization goals linked to external professional measures and neoliberal values— assessable outcomes, metrics, efficiency, economy" (p. 313). And as I argue elsewhere (2010), "The current dominant culture of higher education privileges a model of student learning that can be substantiated in standardized tests and other measures that similarly erase difference and reward conformity to immutable, uninterrogated standards" (p. 251). In short, it can be difficult and demoralizing to hold values in such drastic opposition to what the campus culture values.

And given that many instruction programs deliver instruction only in one-shot sessions, where serious relationship-building with students is nearly impossible, and where time constraints and the demands of learning outcomes often render it impractical to employ any creativity, imagination, or care in instructional approaches, the very structure and system upon which most library instruction programs are based almost sabotage feminist efforts from the start.

But even with these challenges, feminist pedagogy is still important, still possible, still worth pursuing. I argue here and elsewhere (2010) that the marginal status of librarians gives us more freedom to experiment with our pedagogy than regular teaching faculty have, especially if we are not bound by the strictures of the credit-bearing information literacy course. While the one-shot class has its own set of challenges, it also has more flexibility that progressive librarians can take advantage of and subvert for progressive purposes. In a sense, it is better to be on the margins than to be recognized as full citizens of the college or university culture, because it is in the margins that we ironically have more freedom. We may still be answerable to the campus requirements for teaching and learning, but we can also still be answerable to ourselves and our own politics in the classroom.

And in that we are indeed answerable to the campus requirements for teaching and learning, having a robust and rigorous assessment plan is a critical component of feminist approach to library instruction. The next chapter explores feminist approaches to assessment and how they might be enacted in the feminist classroom.

4.

Feminist Assessment

Several years ago, when I was still fairly new in my role as Coordinator of Instruction, I presented assessment results to a group of First Year Seminar instructors at my institution. Specifically, I shared pre-/post-test findings from the quizzes we administered in FYS library instruction sessions. Almost universally, the post-tests showed an increase in correct answers, which, to me, was exciting. The question that showed the most dramatic increase in correct answers was one that asked students to explain the purpose of the Boolean operator AND; this question showed an average 30 point difference on the post-test. I interpreted these overall results as a positive indicator of learning, and I was hoping that these findings would reinforce the importance of FYS library instruction to a group that is sometimes skeptical of the importance of what we do in the library. I was also hoping to legitimize myself and the program as a valid teaching and learning endeavor.

For the most part, my results were well-received, but one faculty member, a professor from the School of Social Sciences, was dismissive. "These results are not statistically significant," she sniffed disdainfully. I was crushed but pretended that I was really interested in her point. I asked her what statistical methods I should use to determine significance. She made a few suggestions, which I made noises about trying, but really I had no idea how to go about statistical analysis. I still don't. I come from a humanities background, which did not require statistics, and my library school program did not require statistics. Quantitative analysis is not my strong suit; I can barely calculate percentages. However, I still thought that my results mattered, even if they were rejected and scorned by one faculty member.

This impulse to use assessment results, especially quantitative, statistically significant findings, to legitimize teaching and learning is not unique to library instruction. It comes from a culture of assessment that is prevalent in higher education. Ewell (1991) and Huba and Freed (2000) trace the origins of the assessment movement in higher education in the United States. Ewell observes that there are two main roots of the assessment movement: an internal movement that originated from within the academy, and an external movement that derived from state and national interests. The internal aspect of the movement dates from the mid-1980s, when four separate reports were issued calling for reform in higher education. These reports were *Access to Quality Undergraduate Education* (1985), *Involvement in Learning* (1984), *Integrity in the College Curriculum* (1985), and *To Reclaim a Legacy* (1984). As Ewell notes, "Each report, in its own way, made a basic connection between assessment and educational reform" (p. 78). The external focus on assessment was spawned by the accountability movement within state governance, which was concerned with return on investment of public funds. Here, too, a series of reports were issued in the mid-1980s, including *Transforming the State Role in Undergraduate Education* (1986) and *Time for Results* (1986): "Consistent with prior academic improvement reports, these documents highlighted the use of assessment as a tool of reform" (Ewell, 1991, p. 80). Thus, both within the academy and outside it, the call for assessment became a method of reform in higher education.

In addition to echoing Ewell's genealogy of the assessment movement, Huba and Freed also trace its origins to the late 1980s quality improvement movement in the corporate sector. Just as American businesses turned to quality improvement in order to compete with foreign counterparts, so, too, did higher education in the United States: "Likewise, colleges and universities pursued continuous improvement because of competition for students, the need to reduce costs and improve quality of services, and the desire to enhance learning" (p. 18). This move to a corporate business model is still visible today in higher education, where, in some institutional cultures, students are viewed as customers, and tuition dollars are viewed as revenue streams.

The assessment movement continued to evolve through the 1990s. In 1998, Title IV of the Higher Education Amendments mandated that institutions receiving federal funds must have an "outcomes assessment plan that includes a review of the institution's success with respect to student achievement" (Gratch-Lindauer, 2002, p. 14). This requirement to assess student learning is also echoed in regional accrediting organization standards, most of which underwent revision in the late 1990s and early 2000s. A 2002 review of regional accreditation standards revealed that "the emphasis on assessing student learning and other outcomes is generally stronger with those associations that have been or are currently undergoing revision since 1998." (Gratch-Lindauer, 2002, p. 15). It is at this point that information literacy and the role of the academic library in teaching and learning starts to become part of the accreditation picture (Gratch-Lindauer, 2002).

At around the same time that regional accrediting bodies started recognizing the role the academic library plays in teaching and learning, Iannuzzi (1999) argued that the academic library needed to more strongly articulate its role in teaching and learning, questioning why information literacy assessment was so difficult and challenging, and advocating for a model of library assessment that places student learning at the center. Soon after this, the Association of College and Research Libraries (ACRL) formalized the definition of information literacy and promulgated competency standards in 2000. Very little guidance was provided in this document, however, regarding how to assess information literacy. In what amounts to four paragraphs, the Competencies document advises, among other things, "developing local methods for measuring student learning in the context of an institution's unique mission" (ACRL, 2000). This failure to provide more specific guidance is both curious and liberating. On the one hand, it is puzzling that this official institutionalization of an important concept would fail to articulate ways in which information literacy learning might be assessed. On the other hand, its relative silence on assessment frees academic librarians to develop methods that are customized to specific learning concepts and environments. In a sense, the lack of guidance about assessment challenges the monolithic view of information literacy the standards themselves promote.

Following this official endorsement was an explosion in the professional literature concerning information literacy. However, prior to the development and promotion of ACRL's official definition of information literacy, assessing information literacy instruction, or, its earlier form, bibliographic instruction, was still a concept of relevance in the literature. A 1995 review of the literature by Bober, Poulin, and Vileno analyzed "the evaluation of bibliographic instruction in academic libraries from 1980-1993" (p. 53). Citing the importance of evaluating a program's effectiveness and being accountable to administration, Bober, Poulin and Vileno observe that evaluation of library instruction "can be a vital key to academic libraries' survival in difficult economic times" (p. 55). This emphasis on economic viability is an interesting one, one that reinforces the dominant culture's capitalist perspective on education as a series of investments that must yield a measurable return on investment.

The literature also began to reflect a growing culture of assessment in academic libraries, emphasizing the importance of assessment as an ongoing process, not just something that is hurriedly accomplished in anticipation of an accreditation visit (Maki, 2002). In short, the information literacy assessment movement can be linked to the general assessment movement in higher education, as well as the increased popularity of strategic planning in higher education, and the development of the actual concept of information literacy (Meulemans, 2002). This culture of assessment is certainly dominant in academic librarianship today. There is increased emphasis on proving the value of the academic library to its relevant stakeholders. The ACRL Value of Academic Libraries initiative is one such example of this obsessive fixation on "proving" that the academic library provides tangible, measurable impact.

Feminist assessment: What do feminist and critical pedagogies have to say?

The literature on assessment in the field of feminist pedagogy is disproportionately small. The literature tends to focus primarily on what feminist pedagogy is and what it looks like rather than addressing how the learning outcomes of a classroom taught using feminist pedagogy might be measured or evaluated. This gap in the literature probably exists due to an impression that assessment is somehow anti-feminist, that assessment is counter to the learner-centered, consciousness-raising focus of feminist pedagogy. As Clifford (2002) notes, the lack of attention to assessment in the feminist pedagogy literature may be due to the potential incongruity between the notions of feminism and assessment: "This limited interest in assessment may reflect the contradictory nature of the word 'assessment' attached to the concept of 'feminist'" (p. 109). Assessment suggests that there is one answer to a question, that there are definitive things that we want learners to know that can be quantified and verified. Feminist pedagogy is open to multiple forms of knowledge, holding that there can be many answers to any one question, and seeks to transform the patriarchal banking model of learning that encourages students to uncritically regurgitate what they have learned.

But I contend that a feminist assessment is possible. Feminist assessment is guided by the principles of feminist pedagogy. It is learner-centered and diverse and validates differing perspectives and voices. It challenges the power relations that govern traditional assessment methods. It seeks to bring about social change and feminist activism. Feminist assessment is inherently reflective, and reflection itself is a feminist act. It questions traditional modes of assessment and challenges the power relations that define and dictate the banking model. The authority of the teacher is decentered in favor of repositioning the student at the center. It seeks to disrupt the patriarchal model of teaching and learning that validates the status quo. Instead of relying on standards that erase difference and individuality, feminist assessment acknowledges the uniqueness of each learner and measures learning in a way that validates this uniqueness. Traditional classroom assessment techniques are modified in ways that are explicitly feminist. Learning outcomes include consciousness-raising about feminist issues such as gender inequity, racism, and homophobia.

In contrast, traditional assessment reinforces and reifies the patriarchal power structures that govern society. It facilitates and validates the banking model of learning, where learners are not encouraged to think critically but are instead rewarded for restating and reiterating the knowledge that teachers deposit into them. Teachers are the ultimate authority and source of wisdom and truth. Learners are voiceless and powerless. Standardized tests are the ultimate in traditional assessment. Standards are formed in the context of patriarchal values without regard to the reality of diversity and individual needs. Assessment has a great deal of power. Assessment in the form of grades has the power to hold a student back or allow him or her to advance. Assessment in higher education determines whether a student persists and graduates with a degree. Assessment is how an institution remains accountable to accrediting bodies, which, in turn, legitimizes the institution. The institution itself, without any critical perspective, as well as the learning outcomes, are reproduced and reinforced through teaching and learning. That is, the institution reifies what it considers knowledge and learning, and this is repeated ad infinitum through assessment cycles.

In the library instruction classroom, traditional assessment takes the form of knowledge tests, classroom assessment techniques, and program assessment strategies. The Project SAILS from Kent State University standardized test is one assessment instrument that has emerged as a dominant method of assessing information literacy. It is a multiple-choice knowledge test based on the ACRL standards for information literacy. It accepts the ACRL standards uncritically and reproduces their definitive power.

The early examples in the literature on feminist assessment examine what feminist assessment is and how it is characterized. Hutchings (1992) examines the assessment agenda in the context of the women's studies movement and describes what feminist assessment looks like. Feminist assessment, according to Hutchings, eschews standardized testing and privileges student involvement in the assessment process. Hutchings also points to the power relations that are inherent to the assessment process, and how feminist assessment questions those power structures: "We also assume there is politics underlying issues of knowledge, and it causes us to ask about the uses to which assessment will be put. Who has the power to determine the questions? What methods are most appropriate to embrace the many voices and ways of speaking? What methods help reveal the unspoken?" (p. 24). This emphasis on questioning the power relations that govern knowledge production is echoed by Shapiro (1992): "Feminist assessment is open to questioning how assessment previously has been carried out, including all paradigms, traditions, approaches, and instruments" (p. 31). Shapiro also notes that feminist assessment is student-centered, participatory, and context-specific. Shapiro then makes an important point about the necessity that feminist assessment be aligned with feminist activism, a defining feature of feminist pedagogy: "Rather than an abstraction floating without any ties to the concrete, feminist assessment is action-oriented and encourages social change to be achieved as an outcome of the process" (p. 34).

This emphasis on the power of feminist assessment to change lives and change the world is examined in a later instance in the literature, which looks at a specific form of direct, authentic assessment. Clifford (2002) examines personal journals, which are written about education students' coursework, as a possible feminist assessment technique: "The purpose of the journal is to encourage the student to become aware of their own learning, the way they reconstruct new knowledge in the light of their existing knowledge and experience, and to assess their own development" (p. 110). The goals for this form of assessment are consistent with feminist pedagogical principles, which privilege student voice, student knowledge, reflection, and consciousness-raising. Ultimately, Clifford found that while the concept of journal keeping as a feminist assessment technique has a sound basis in feminist pedagogical principles, the journals themselves did not necessarily yield feminist reflections or analyses. Clifford notes,

"However, a focus on issues reflecting a wider context of social justice, for example, sexism and racism, was mostly only salient in the journals of the lecturers whose courses overtly involved these issues" (p. 109). That is, if the subject matter of the course related to social justice, racism, sexism, or other feminist issues, then the student reflection in the journal mirrored this content. This example validates this book's earlier assertion that feminist forms of pedagogy cannot just be feminist in theory; the content of the learning must also be feminist for the pedagogy to have an impact.

Feminist pedagogy is embedded in a broader critical pedagogy, so it is worthwhile to also turn to the literature on critical pedagogy assessment in general, in order to get a fuller picture of the possibilities of feminist assessment. As defined in Chapter 2, "Pedagogy focuses on strategies, techniques, and approaches used to facilitate learning. Critical pedagogy is also interested in learning facilitation, but is primarily concerned with exposing the interests involved in the production and dissemination of knowledge" ("Pedagogy/critical pedagogy," 2007). Thus, turning to the critical pedagogy literature for additional perspective makes sense in this context.

Like feminist pedagogy, critical pedagogy and assessment seeks to disrupt the traditional power relations between student and teacher, privilege student voices, and expose the oppressive dominant culture so that society can be transformed. Price, O'Donovan, and Rust (2007) describe a social-constructivist model that called for student participation and engagement with the assessment process, from developing evaluation criteria to focus groups to peer review to a "feedback workshop," where students were encouraged to actively engage with comments provided on their work. The goal was to make explicit knowledge that is often left hidden or mysterious. Reynolds and Trehan (2000) provide a critical perspective on assessment that uses participative assessment as a mode of evaluation. Echoing feminist pedagogy's reluctance to engage with the hierarchical structures that are inherent in assessment, Reynolds and Trehan note, "More than any other aspect of education, assessment embodies power relations between the institution and its students, with tutors as custodians of the institution's rules and practices" (p. 268). Their use of participative assessment, which is defined as "a process in which students and tutors share, to some degree, the responsibility for making evaluations and judgments about students' written work, gaining insight into how such judgments are made and finding appropriate ways to communicate them," (p. 270) subverts the traditional hierarchical power structures that govern the assessment process and places learners at the center of the process.

But does this student-centered approach actually have an impact? Tan (2004) examines whether self-assessment, often used as a form of critical assessment, actually serves to empower students: "The student's lack of power is framed as an impediment to their learning and student self-assessment is commonly advocated as an opportunity for students to gain a measure of power or control in the assessment process. The assumption is that student participation in the assessment process enhances student empowerment" (p. 651). This assumption needs to be examined, however, according to Tan, who argues that it is insufficient to merely tell students to assess themselves; instructors must help learners understand to enact autonomy in their assessment, which is in direct contradiction to everything they know about education thus far.

Finally, the critical and feminist suspicion of assessment in general is echoed in a Marxian examination of the accountability movement, which is a component of the assessment movement looking specifically at state-mandated methods of defining and controlling student learning. This critique does not provide alternative, critical approaches to assessment, as the examples in the feminist and critical literature do. There still is value, however, in conceptual critiques, in that they provide alternative perspectives and approaches that can inform practical approaches. This particular critique challenges the concept of assessment itself by providing a startling glimpse into the potentially destructive power of assessment:

> Dominant trends in educational accountability facilitate a violent reification of human consciousness and creativity, serve to inscribe neocolonial assumptions of white supremacy and derive from a repressive juridical rationality that constitutes students as indebted to the capitalist system by which they are exploited (De Lissovoy & Giroux, 2003, p. 132).

This helps reinforce the feminist critique of assessment; namely, that an uncritical approach to assessment perpetuates the oppression of the dominant culture. It also brings to bear another perspective on the dangers of uncritical assessment: that the capitalist system that invests in education expects a return on investment, and the reduction of education to a commodified transaction results in "no instant of schooling [...] available to its alternative conceptualization as a 'practice of freedom'" (p. 141). This is a rather hopeless perspective, but I would argue that the feminist perspective, while recognizing the same destructive logics that does the Marxian analysis, still is open to hope and the possibility of liberatory education. The feminist ethic of care, which is detailed more specifically in Chapter 2, emphasizes the role of relationships and affect in teacher/student relationships. This kind of caring relationship-building has the power to undo the violence and oppression of the dominant educational system that the Marxian analysis describes.

What implications do these approaches have for information literacy and library instruction assessment? And why should we press on, if critical approaches are more challenging and difficult and emotionally exhausting? It is worth it because of the power to change and transform the world.

Having hope in the transformative power of "education as the practice of freedom" makes it worth pursuing feminist pedagogical methods in the library instruction classroom.

The next section examines common forms of information literacy assessment and then envisions the feminist and critical potential for these techniques.

Feminist Approaches to Information Literacy Assessment

I'm reminded once again of the story I told at the beginning of this chapter, where I tried to legitimize myself as a teacher and validate my program through knowledge quiz assessment findings. My feelings were bruised when my findings were rejected, yes, but it also turned out to be one of my many moments of *conscientização* as an aspiring critical and feminist teacher. As I reflected further on the experience, I had to remember that it's not always about me. Yes, I want people to believe in me and my knowledge as a teacher. But ultimately, it's about the students and their learning and what I can do to facilitate their learning.

Focusing on students and their learning informed one of my most feminist moments as an instruction librarian, where I held a focus group with a group of honors students to get their perspective on an information literacy assessment rubric that I planned to use to evaluate their research portfolios. As I have outlined elsewhere (2010), I sought student feedback on the rubric and used their feedback to modify the rubric. I also had them review the learning outcomes I use in library instruction sessions and made some changes accordingly. This was a time-consuming process, however, and not all instruction librarians have the luxury of time or embeddedness in academic programs on campus. So something as simple as beginning a session with questions such as "What should we learn in this session today?" can be a feminist response to the time constraints faced by most librarian instructors.

Given the arguments for assessment that is learner-centered, contextualized, driven by something other than uncritical adherence to standards, here are some strategies that challenge the uncritical approach while still providing useful snapshots of student learning and effective teaching. They are all also possible to enact within the time and structural constraints faced by instruction librarians.

Classroom Assessment Techniques

There are a number of different techniques an instruction librarian can employ when assessing information literacy in the classroom. Classroom assessment techniques (CAT) tend to be formative methods of assessment. According to Radcliff et al. (2007), "Formative assessment can be conducted while students are learning in order to gauge that they are learning. It can provide valuable feedback that can be used to improve instruction" (p. 14). Formative assessment measures ongoing learning in progress, while summative assessment measures the final result of learning. CATs are practical, action-oriented, and provide a glimpse into what students know and understand (Radcliff et al., 2007).

Knowledge tests are one form of a CAT. Usually taking the form of objective multiple-choice questions, knowledge tests do just that: assess what learners know. Knowledge tests assess the cognitive domain of learning (Radcliff et al., 2007). Librarians can employ knowledge tests at the end of the session to see what students learned, or they can deliver a knowledge test in a pre-/post-test format, which allows librarians to more easily see the impact of instruction on students. If the number of correct answers increases on the post-test, it is safe to assume that some sort of learning happened during the library instruction session. Knowledge test questions should be mapped to the learning outcomes defined for the session, and it can be flexible enough to use in multiple sessions.

Another CAT is the defining features matrix. This technique also addresses the cognitive domain of learning. According to Radcliff et al. (2007), "This tool can be used in situations when you want students to demonstrate that they understand the differences or similarities between concepts, resources, or methodologies" (p. 40). A defining features matrix might ask students to distinguish between scholarly or popular periodicals, or the library catalog and article databases.

Directed paraphrasing is another example of a CAT. This technique asks students to restate or explain the material addressed during a library instruction session (Radcliff et al., 2007). This is a longer version of the one sentence summary, another CAT that allows students to explain what they have learned. And finally, another CAT instruction librarians might employ is the one-minute paper or the muddiest point paper. This reflective exercise asks students to report one thing they learned during that session, and one thing that still remains unclear and about which the student has questions (Radcliff et al., 2007).

Can a CAT be critical and feminist? At first glance, knowledge tests in particular seem especially patriarchal and rigid in form. Objective multiple-choice questions do not provide space for student voice or experiential knowledge. The defining features matrix is another structured CAT that seems inflexible and uncritical at first as well. But when deployed in conjunction with a tool like the directed paraphrasing, the minute paper, or the muddiest point, these inflexible tools are more amenable to critical approaches. Thus, a feminist approach to classroom assessment must necessarily involve more than one assessment tool. Directed paraphrasing, the minute paper, and the muddiest point provide learners with the opportunity to assess their own learning in their own words, and valuing the voice of the student is a central feminist pedagogical principle. These methods are less rigid and structured than the knowledge test, and their very nature thwarts the notion that there is only one answer or one way of knowing and experiencing the world. These techniques can be made more critical and more feminist by adding an element of self-assessment and personal reflection to them. For example, the one-minute paper, directed paraphrasing, or one sentence summary might ask students to reflect on what they learned and to evaluate their learning and performance during the instruction session.

Performance Assessment Techniques

The assessment of student performance is considered direct, authentic, formative assessment. As described by Radcliff et al. (2007), "performance assessments allow students to demonstrate what they can do, as opposed to describing what they know" (p. 116). An alternative to the knowledge test, performance assessment evaluates a student's research process, such as a research journal or portfolio, or a research product, like a research paper or annotated bibliography. Performance assessments can be scored using a checklist, a rating scale, or a rubric (Radcliff et al., 2007).

The reflective research portfolio has great feminist potential. It is student-centered and values reflection and the student's contributions to a body of knowledge. It values process in addition to product, provides space for student expression, and challenges traditional teacher/student power relations by empowering students to choose how to represent themselves for evaluation.

The problem with the research portfolio, however, is that it is more suitable for credit-bearing courses, which closes off the possibility for using it in one-shot sessions, which is still how a great deal of library instruction is conducted. Feminist assessment is still possible in the one-shot session though the use of critical CATs as described earlier, but what does this suggest about the library instruction profession when the way many of us deliver instruction is not fully amenable to critical modes of pedagogy? It is, perhaps, suggestive of our marginal status, where we are relegated to occasional one-offs and slotted into already overflowing curricula.

Perhaps one way of attempting the portfolio in a one-shot session is an alternative project that I call the mini-portfolio. I imagine this as a collection of the artifacts from that single one-shot session, such as a completed worksheet, a research log, and a reflective one-minute paper, all assembled electronically in such a way that both student and librarian would have access to it. The librarian could then evaluate the mini-portfolio contents and provide commentary about the student's research process for the student to see. It is possible that this could be accomplished via librarian presence in the course management system software. While it may not have the lasting impact as does a long-term portfolio project, I see this as one way in which this assessment tool can be adapted for the feminist one-shot session.

Surveys, Interviewing, and Focus Groups

Other assessment methods include the survey, the interview, and focus groups (Radcliff et al., 2007). Surveys, interviews, and focus groups all can address the cognitive domain of learning as well as the affective. A survey might seek information about what students think and feel about their library instruction experience. They are easier to administer than a focus group or interview, and if constructed with closed-ended questions, they are comparatively easy to analyze. Library instruction surveys can be feminist in that they can ask questions about satisfaction with library instruction experiences, or perceptions of librarian helpfulness, all of which serve to validate student voices and input.

Interviews and focus groups are more difficult to conduct and analyze, but are more open to explicit feminist potential than the survey. Soliciting volunteers to participate is perhaps one of the biggest challenges of conducting an interview or a focus group about library instruction, but if a librarian is successful in recruiting participants, these tools are very receptive to feminist critique. The interviewer or focus group leader can ask participants questions about information literacy concepts, and the feedback students provide can give librarians a new and different perspective on how students regard the library instruction experience.

In a sense, the mere act of asking questions in these formats can be read as feminist. Seeking the student voice, validating student knowledge, and displaying an ethic of care are all feminist pedagogical principles.

All of these assessment strategies have their advantages and drawbacks. Some are more suitable for one-shot sessions, while others are more successful in situations where there is a more long-term relationship with the learner. Like any form of teaching, assessment strategies and results should be used to thoughtfully reflect on student learning and whether the pedagogy is enabling the learning and meeting learning goals, whether the goals are traditional or critical. Feminist assessment of information literacy provides a useful and powerful perspective on student learning that takes into account not just information literacy learning but the transformative power of feminist teaching and learning. Some sample classroom assessment techniques can be found in Appendix C.

Conclusion

Or, Loneliness, Caring for Self, Caring for Others

When I was about halfway through writing this book, I was browsing the HQ 1200s looking for a particular book about feminism, and, with that wonderful serendipity that only browsing the stacks can bring, I happened upon a 1976 mass market title called *How to Become an Assertive Woman: The Key to Self-Fulfillment* by Bryna Taubman. Published the year before I was born, the text is careful to distinguish between "aggressiveness" and "assertiveness," and defines "assertiveness" as the "expression of your own feelings, wants and needs, learning to act on them and having respect for the feelings, wants and needs of those around you" (p. 1). The 1970s were a key era for feminism, and it makes sense that a book seeking to rectify gender inequality would be published in this time. Pointing out that women are socially conditioned to not express their needs or wants, the book provides strategies and tactics to help women get what they want.

While dated, the book still has useful tips for women who want to be more assertive; women of today could still learn from this book. I myself have learned from this book, and I could have used it while writing large portions of the book you are now holding in your hands. Writing *Feminist Pedagogy for Library Instruction* required a kind of confident assertiveness. I could not have written this book if I didn't believe that my voice had value, that I had something to say, that I was smart enough to say it, and that people would want to read it. Taubman's advice, especially her admonition, "Don't put yourself down," came to me at a critical time, one where I was battling writer's block, and her words helped me be assertive enough to finish writing the book.

And now I'm going to be assertive enough to talk to you, the reader, about loneliness. This is not something that people want to talk about, but this profession can be lonely and alienating and isolating for people who think differently, people who aren't valued and represented by the dominant culture. I'll begin by talking about when I was working on my M.A. in English at the University of Louisville in the early 2000s, when I took a summer class that was designed to teach me how to be a teacher. Prior to that class, the only instructional experience I had was working as a peer consultant in the University Writing Center at U of L in the first year of my graduate teaching assistantship. The second year of my assistantship required me to teach first year composition classes, and hence, there was the summer class to teach me how to be a teacher. There are lots of things that I learned and still retain from that class, but one of the things that stands out to me the most is learning about Paulo Freire and the banking method of teaching and learning. Freire's vision of a teacher was the kind of teacher I wanted to be, I realized, the kind of teacher who resists the notion that the teacher is the source of all truth and knowledge, and that students are passive vessels waiting to be filled with that knowledge. I was inspired and energized by this notion.

And then I actually started teaching. And I was distressed to learn that for the most part, my students *wanted* to be passive vessels. They *wanted* me to be the source of authority and wisdom. I wasn't experienced or confident enough to try to change this situation, to try to forge ahead with critical teaching practices anyway. I felt lonely and confused and doubted whether I was meant to be a teacher at all.

As of this writing, I've been an instruction librarian for seven years now, and for many of those years, I've continued feeling lonely and alienated. I've felt lonely because the dominant culture of instruction librarianship and information literacy does not always speak to me and my values. For example, at the ALA Annual Conference in 2008 in Anaheim, I walked out of a session, shaking with anger and righteous indignation. I had gone to a Library Instruction Round Table session, which purported to be about "energizing library instruction." When I walked in and saw people blowing bubbles, this should have been the first sign that something was amiss. I sat down and paged through the sheaf of handouts provided and tried to not worry that there was some sappy poem in there about love. I tried not to worry about the PowerPoint slides flashing on the screen before the session started. The slides were full of tidbits of non-interesting trivia—I seriously did not come to the session to learn that the number one product that Wal-Mart sells the most of is bananas—and there were also some embarrassing grammatical errors on the slides, too. One slide in the presentation said something about losing weight or losing inches, but I assumed—or I hoped—that it was some sort of stupid punny jokey gimmicky thing about instruction. I tried valiantly to counter the resistance I felt building steadily inside of me. *C'mon,* I told myself. *Give it a chance! Try to have fun! Have a better attitude!* There were so many red flags pointing to intellectual bankruptcy, but still I remained, forcing myself to give it a chance.

And then! I noticed a pamphlet on the floor. It had fallen off the seat when I sat down. I was totally stunned and appalled to discover a pamphlet promoting a brand of diet pills. That slide about losing inches? Not a joke. *It was an actual pitch for a series of weight loss products being sold to me at a session at a professional library conference.* I looked at the back of the pamphlet, where the salesperson's name was listed, and it was a

woman's name with the same last name as the speaker. I sus-
pect that it was his wife, and that the speaker--Andrew
Sanderbeck of People-Connect Institute--thought it was perfectly fine to try to sell weight loss products at a session at a
professional conference. He was sorely mistaken. On what
planet is it acceptable to allow a program speaker to sell
weight loss products to an audience of professional adults at
a professional conference?

I registered an extremely strongly-worded complaint to
one of the session organizers. She claimed that they didn't
know that he was going to hand out those pamphlets, and
that I should disregard it and throw away. I could not believe
that this was her response, which was wholly unprofessional,
unacceptable, and inadequate. I quickly scribbled an equally
strongly-worded comment on the evaluation form and thrust
it into her face.

I went to that session to learn about improving the way I
do library instruction. I did not go there to receive a bottle of
bubbles. I didn't appreciate being patronized. I am a professional and intelligent adult, and I did not care to be associated
with a group that did not find it unacceptable that the program speaker saw this session as a chance to sell us diet pills.

Years later, I still can't believe that this actually happened.
I still remember how alienating and isolating and depressing it
felt that the Library Instruction Round Table, which was
supposed to represent me and my interests, thought this was
acceptable. This is an extreme example, I concede, but it represents so vividly why I feel like I don't belong in instruction
librarianship sometimes. Maybe I'm just one of those humor-
less feminists people complain about, but when I talk about
library instruction, I'm serious. I don't want to be invited to
blow bubbles. And I definitely don't want to be sold diet
pills. I want to talk about teaching and learning with the respect and gravity that I think they warrant. This is not to suggest that I think teaching and learning should always be a so-

ber endeavor. I think there can be fun and levity in the classroom, of course. I just think that it should be intelligent fun,
fun that is framed and informed by theory, not bubble wands.
I want practical guidance and teaching ideas, yes, but why
does it have to be articulated in the rhetoric of a cookbook?
Why are we so preoccupied with turning learning into something silly, or a game?

All of this is a long-winded way of saying that being a serious person, being a theory-minded person, being a feminist
in a profession that does not always value those things can be
lonely. You, too, might feel lonely if you try to practice feminist teaching. The thing about feminist teaching is that you
may be doing so in a context where feminism is not widely
understood, accepted, or embraced. And it is also exhausting
to have to explain yourself to people who don't get it. There
will indeed be people who don't get it, who don't know what
it means to teach in a feminist way, or what it means to care
for the souls of students. Once, when I explained what I was
writing about—this book—to a colleague, she laughed, like it
was funny, like feminism is a joke and I was doing something
stupid and silly and weird. To people who don't get it, feminist teaching is stupid and silly and weird, and you just have
to accept this and move on and not take it personally. You
can and could try to educate others about what you're doing
and why, but don't internalize it if your explanations go nowhere.

Actively caring for the souls of students also requires that
we care for our own souls first. We have to secure our own
oxygen mask before helping others secure theirs. A kind of
self-care that I've found invaluable is what Rosanne Bane in
her book *Around the Writer's Block* calls Process Time. Process
Time is creative free play for the sake of play; no product or
end result is expected or desired. Process Time can take the
form of coloring, painting, playing with clay, freewriting, or
any other creative endeavor. What does this have to do with

teaching, let alone writing? Process Time feeds your soul, your desires, your inner self. And feeding your inner self is essential when you're in a profession that feels isolating.

You can also feed your inner self by keeping a reflective teaching journal. You can also feed your inner self by engaging with like-minded people and words that speak to you. Read some bell hooks and let her words sink in. Read the library literature to see who is talking about critical stuff and make connections to those people. It wasn't until I was a practicing instruction librarian two years after my graduate study in English and I read James Elmborg's 2006 article "Critical Information Literacy: Implications for Instructional Practice" that I realized that the critical ideas that once excited me might possibly have a place in librarianship. Write to me, the author of this book. I'll talk to you about how it feels to try to teach in a feminist way and try to encourage you. Seek encouragement from those who matter to you and try not to worry too much about those who don't.

Most of all, have hope. Critical feminist teaching matters, even if people try to discourage you or question what you're doing, even if in the context of ALA Annual sessions your ideas seem foreign and out of place. Be assertive and confident. Don't put yourself down. Have hope for yourself and your students and for a world where feminist teaching makes a tangible difference. Have hope.

References

Accardi, M. T. (2010). Teaching against the grain: Critical assessment in the library classroom. In M. T. Accardi, E. Drabinski, & A. Kumbier (Eds.) *Critical library instruction: Theories and methods* (pp. 251-264). Duluth, MN: Library Juice Press.

Association of College and Research Libraries. (2000). Information Literacy Competency Standards for Higher Education. Retrieved from http://www.ala.org/acrl/standards/informationliteracycompetency

Bass, L. (2012). When care trumps justice: The operationalization of Black feminist caring in educational leadership. *International Journal of Qualitative Studies In Education, 25*(1), 73-87.

Beauboeuf-Lafontant, T. (2002). A womanist experience of caring: Understanding the pedagogy of exemplary Black women teachers. *The Urban Review, 34*(1), 71-86.

Belenky, M. F., Clinchy, B. M., Goldberger, N. R., & Tarule, J. M. (1997). *Women's ways of knowing: The development of self, voice, and mind.* New York: Basic Books.

Bell, S., Morrow, M., & Tastsoglou, E. (1999). Teaching in environments of resistance: Toward a critical, feminist, and antiracist pedagogy. In M. Mayberry & E. C. Rose (Eds.), *Meeting the challenge: Innovative feminist pedagogies in action,* (pp. 23-48). New York: Routledge.

Bignell, K. C. (1996). Building feminist praxis out of feminist pedagogy: The importance of student perspectives. *Women's Studies International Forum, 19*(3), 315-325.

Broidy, E. (2007). Gender and the politics of the classroom: Reflections on bringing the library into the classroom. *Library Trends, 56*(2): 494-508.

Bober, C., Poulin, S., & Vileno, L. (1995). Evaluating library instruction in academic libraries: A critical review of the literature. *Reference Librarian*, (51/52), 53.

Booth, C. (2011). *Reflective teaching, effective learning: Instructional literacy for library educators*. Chicago: American Library Association.

Brown, J. (1992). Theory or practice: What exactly is feminist pedagogy? *The Journal of General Education, 41*, 51-63.

Carillo, E. C. (2007). "Feminist" teaching/teaching "feminism." *Feminist Teacher, 18*(1): 28-40.

Chow, E. N., Fleck, C., Gang-Hua, F., Joseph, J., & Lyter, D. M. (2003). Exploring critical feminist pedagogy: Infusing dialogue, participation, and experience in teaching and learning. *Teaching Sociology, 31*(3), 259-275.

Clifford, V. A. (2002). Does the use of journals as a form of assessment put into practice principles of feminist pedagogy? *Gender and Education, 14*(2), 109-121.

Crabtree, R. D., Sapp, D. A., and Licona, A. C. (2009). (Eds.) *Feminist pedagogy: Looking back to move forward*. Baltimore: Johns Hopkins University Press.

Crawley, S. L., Lewis, J. E., & Mayberry, M. (2008). Introduction—Feminist pedagogies in action: Teaching beyond disciplines. *Feminist Teacher, 19*(1): 1-12.

De Lissovoy, N. & Giroux, H. (2003). Educational 'accountability' and the violence of capital: a Marxian reading. *Journal Of Education Policy, 18*(2), 131.

Duncan, K. & Stasio, M. (2001). Surveying feminist pedagogy: A measurement, an evaluation, and an affirmation.
*Feminist Teacher, (13)*3: 225-239.

Eisenhower, C. & Smith, D. (2010). The library as "stuck
place": Critical pedagogy in the corporate university. In M. T.
Accardi, E. Drabinski, & A. Kumbier (Eds.) *Critical library
instruction: Theories and methods* (pp. 305-317). Duluth, MN: Library Juice Press.

Ellsworth, E. (1992). Why doesn't this feel empowering?
Working through the repressive myths of critical pedagogy.
In C. Luke & J. Gore (Eds.), *Feminisms and critical pedagogy,* (pp.
90-119), New York: Routledge.

Eubanks, D. L., Murphy, S. T., & Mumford, M. D. (2010).
Intuition as an influence on creative problem-solving: The
effects of intuition, positive affect, and training. *Creativity Research Journal, 22*(2), 170-184.

Ewell, P. (1991). To capture the ineffable: New forms of assessment in higher education. *Review of Research in Education* ,
75-125.

"Feminism." (2001). In *World of Sociology.* Retrieved from
http://www.credoreference.com.

Fisher, B. (1981). What is feminist pedagogy? *Radical Teacher,
18*, 20-24.

Fisher, B. M. (2001). *No angel in the classroom: Teaching through
feminist discourse.* Lanham, MD: Rowman & Littlefield.

Freedman, E. B. (1990). Small group pedagogy: Consciousness raising in conservative times. *NWSA Journal, 2*(4), 603.

Friedensohn, D. (1997). Women's lives, 1945-1955: Personal
narratives and the pedagogy of intergenerational interview-
ing. *American Studies, 38*(3), 119.

Freire, P. (1970). *Pedagogy of the oppressed*. New York: Continuum.

Gibson, C. (2008). The history of information literacy. In C. N. Cox & E. B. Lindsay (Eds.) *Information literacy instruction handbook* (pp. 10-25). Chicago: Association of College and Research Libraries.

Gilchrist, D. & Zald, A. (2008). Instruction and program design through assessment. In C. N. Cox & E. B. Lindsay (Eds.) *Information literacy instruction handbook* (pp. 164-192). Chicago: Association of College and Research Libraries.

Giroux, J. B. (1989). Feminist theory as pedagogical practice. *Contemporary Education, 61*(1), 6-10.

Gore, J. (1992). What we can do for you! What can "we" do for "you"? Struggling over empowerment in critical in feminist pedagogy. In C. Luke & J. Gore (Eds.) *Feminisms and critical pedagogy* (pp. 54-73). New York: Routledge.

Gratch-Lindauer, B. (2002). Comparing the regional accreditation standards: Outcomes assessment and other trends. *Journal of Academic Librarianship, 28*(1/2), 14.

Harding, S. G. (1986). *The science question in feminism*. Ithaca: Cornell University Press.

Hayes, E. (1989). Insights from women's experiences for teaching and learning. *New Directions for Continuing Education, 43*, 55-66.

Hoffmann, F. L. & Stake, J. E. (1998). Feminist pedagogy in theory and practice: An empirical investigation. *NWSA Journal, 10*(1), 79-97.

hooks, b. (1994). *Teaching to transgress: Education as the practice of freedom*. New York: Routledge.

Huba, M. E., & Freed, J. E. (2000). *Learner-centered assessment on college campuses: Shifting the focus from teaching to learning.* Boston: Allyn and Bacon.

Hutchings, P. (1992). The assessment movement and feminism: Connection or collision? In Musil, C. T. (Ed). *Students at the center: Feminist assessment* (pp. 17-38). Washington, D.C: Association of American Colleges.

Iannuzzi, P. (1999). We are teaching, but are they learning: accountability, productivity, and assessment. *Journal Of Academic Librarianship, 25*(4), 304.

Ladenson, S. (2010). Paradigm shift: Utilizing critical feminist pedagogy in library instruction. In M. T. Accardi, E. Drabinski, & A. Kumbier (Eds.) *Critical library instruction: Theories and methods* (pp. 105-112). Duluth, MN: Library Juice Press.

Lambert, C., & Parker, A. (2006). Imagination, hope and the positive face of feminism: Pro/feminist pedagogy in "post" feminist times?. *Studies in Higher Education, 31*, 4, 469-482.

Maher, F. (1985). Classroom pedagogy and the new scholarship on women. In M. Culley & C. Portugues (Eds.) *Gendered subjects: The dynamics of feminist teaching* (pp. 28-48). Boston: Routledge.

Maher, F. A. (1987). Toward a richer theory of feminist pedagogy: A comparison of "liberation" and "gender" models for teaching and learning. *Journal of Education, 169*(3), 91-100.

Maki, P. L. (2002). Developing an assessment plan to learn about student learning. *Journal Of Academic Librarianship, 28*(1/2), 8.

McGuinness, C. (2011). *Becoming confident teachers: A guide for academic librarians.* Oxford: Chandos Publishing.

Mellon, C. (1986), Library anxiety: A grounded theory and its development. *College & Research Libraries 47* (2): 160–165

Meulemans, Y. (2002). Assessment city: The past, present, and future state of information literacy assessment. *College & Undergraduate Libraries, 9*(2), 61.

Noddings, N. (1988). An ethic of caring and its implications for instructional arrangements. *American Journal of Education, 96(*2), 215-230.

Noddings, N. (1992). *The Challenge to Care in Schools: An Alternative Approach to Education.* New York: Teachers College Press.

Parry, S. C. (1996). Feminist pedagogy and techniques for the changing classroom. *Women's Studies Quarterly, 24*(3/4), 45-54.

"Pedagogy/critical pedagogy." (2007). In *The Social Science Jargon-Buster.* Retrieved from http://credoreference.com/entry/sageukssjb/pedagogy_critical_pedagogy.

Personal Narratives Group. (1989). Origins. In J. W. Barbre & Personal Narratives Group. *Interpreting women's lives: Feminist theory and personal narratives* (p. 3-15). Bloomington: Indiana University Press.

Price, M., O'Donovan, B., & Rust, C. (2007). Putting a social-constructivist assessment process model into practice: building the feedback loop into the assessment process through peer review. *Innovations In Education & Teaching International, 44*(2), 143-152.

Radcliff, C.J., et al. (2007). *A practical guide to information literacy assessment for academic librarians.* Westport, CT: Libraries Unlimited.

Rea, B. D. (2001). Finding our balance: The investigation and clinical application of intuition. *Psychotherapy: Theory, Research, Practice, Training, 38*(1), 97-106.

Reynolds, M., & Trehan, K. (2000). Assessment: a critical perspective. *Studies In Higher Education, 25*(3), 267-278.

Sandell, R. (1991). The liberating relevance of feminist pedagogy. *Studies in Art Education, 32*(3), 178-187.

Scanlon, J. (1993). Keeping our activist selves alive in the classroom: Feminist pedagogy and political activism. *Feminist Teacher, 7*(2), 8-8.

Schniedewind, N. (1987). Feminist values: Guidelines for teaching methodology in women's studies. In I. Shor (Ed.) *Freire for the classroom: A sourcebook for liberatory teaching* (pp. 170-179). Portsmouth, NH: Boynton/Cook.

Shapiro, J. P. (1992). What is feminist assessment? In Musil, C. T. (Ed). *Students at the center: Feminist assessment* (pp. 29-37). Washington, D.C: Association of American Colleges.

Shor, I. (1987). *Critical teaching and everyday life*. Chicago: University of Chicago Press.

Shor, I. (1992). *Empowering education: Critical teaching for social change*. Chicago: University of Chicago Press.

Shrewsbury, C. (1987). What is feminist pedagogy? *Women's Studies Quarterly, 15*(3/4): 6-14.

Sproles, C., Johnson, A. M., & Farison, L. (2008). What the teachers Are teaching: How MLIS programs are preparing academic librarians for instructional roles. *Journal of Education for Library & Information Science, 49*(3), 195-209.

Stein, G. (1914). *Tender Buttons*. New York: Claire Marie.

Tan, K. K. (2004). Does student self-assessment empower or discipline students? *Assessment & Evaluation In Higher Education, 29*(6), 651-662.

Taubman, B. (1976). *How to become an assertive woman*. New York: Pocket Books.

Thayer-Bacon, B. J., & Bacon, C. S. (1996). Caring professors: A model. *Journal of General Education, 45,* 4, 255-69.

Torrens, K. M. & Riley, J. E. (2004). Students coming to voice: The transformative influences of feminist pedagogies. *The Journal of the Midwest Modern Language Association, 37*(2), 60-73.

Villaverde, L. E. (2008). *Feminist theories and education*. New York: Peter Lang.

Walker, A. (1983). *In search of our mothers' gardens: Womanist prose*. San Diego: Harcourt Brace Jovanovich.

Webb, L. M., Walker, K. L., & Bollis, T. S. (2004). Feminist pedagogy in the teaching of research methods. *Social Research Methodology, 7*(5): 415-428.

Further Reading

Caring and Self-Care

Bane, R. (2012). *Around the writer's block: Using brain science to solve writer's resistance: Including writer's block, procrastination, paralysis, perfectionism, postponing, distractions, self-sabotage, excessive criticism, overscheduling, and endlessly delaying your writing.* New York: Penguin.

Fincher, S. F. (2006). *Coloring mandalas 3: Circles of the sacred feminine.* Boston: Shambhala.

Holbrook, T., Moore, C., & Zoss, M. (2010). Equitable intent: reflections on Universal Design in education as an ethic of care. *Reflective Practice, 11*(5), 681-692.

O'Brien, L. M. (2010). Caring in the ivory tower. *Teaching in Higher Education, 15*(1), 109-115.

Roberts, M. (2010). Toward a theory of culturally relevant critical teacher care: African American teachers' definitions and perceptions of care for African American students. *Journal of Moral Education, 39*(4), 449-467.

Straits, W. (2007). "She's teaching me": Teaching with care in a large lecture course. *College Teaching, 55*(4), 170-175.

Feminist Theory

Bergin, L. A. (2002). Testimony, epistemic difference, and privilege: how feminist epistemology can improve our understanding of the communication of knowledge. *Social Epistemology, 16*(3), 197-213.

Gilligan, C. (1982). *In a different voice: Psychological theory and women's development.* Cambridge, MA: Harvard University Press.

Gilligan, C. (2011). *Joining the resistance.* Cambridge, UK: Polity.

Harding, S. G. (1986). *The science question in feminism.* Ithaca: Cornell University Press.

Harding, S. (2004). Introduction: Standpoint theory as a site of political, philosophic, and scientific debate. In Harding, S. (Ed). *The feminist standpoint theory reader: Intellectual and political controversies* (pp. 1-15). New York, Routledge.

Lee, J. (1997). Women re-authoring their lives through feminist narrative therapy. *Women & Therapy, 20(*3), 1.

Tronto, J. C. (1989). Women and caring: What can feminists learn about morality from caring? In V. Held (Ed.) *Justice and care: Essential readings in feminist ethics* (pp. 101-115). New York: Westview Press.

Pedagogies: Feminist and Critical

Alexander, I. D. (1998). *Learning in other ways: A history of feminist pedagogy in the United States.* (Doctoral dissertation). Retrieved from ProQuest Dissertations and Theses. (9834435).

Beckman, M. M. (1990). Classroom methods mirroring workplace values: Pedagogy of the oppressed, feminist pedagogy and writing across the curriculum. *Review of Radical Political Economics, 22*(2/3), 139.

Birch, M., & Jennings, C. L. (1995). Lifting our morale and inspiring our teaching: Developing a feminist pedagogy retreat. *Feminist Teacher, 9*(1), 28.

Bunch, C. & Pollack, S. (1983). *Learning our way: Essays in feminist education.* Trumansburg, NY: The Crossing Press.

Byrd, D. (2010). *Teaching the "isms": Feminist pedagogy across the disciplines*. Towson, MD: Institute for Teaching and Research on Women.

Culley, M. & Portuges, C. (1985). (Eds.) *Gendered subjects: The dynamics of feminist teaching*. Boston: Routledge.

Davies, S., Lubelska, C., & Quinn, J. (1994). *Changing the subject: Women in higher education*. London: Taylor & Francis.

Gabriel, S. L., & Smithson, I. (1990). *Gender in the classroom: Power and pedagogy*. Urbana: University of Illinois Press.

Gore, J. (1993). *The struggle for pedagogies: Critical and feminist discourses as regimes of truth*. New York: Routledge.

hooks, b. (2000). *Feminism is for everybody: Passionate politics*. Cambridge, MA: South End Press.

hooks, b. (2003). *Teaching community: A pedagogy of hope*. New York: Routledge.

Maher, F. A. (1987). Inquiry teaching and feminist pedagogy. *Social Education, 51*(3), 186-192.

Maher, F. A., & Tetreault, M. K. T. (2001). *The feminist classroom: Dynamics of gender, race, and privilege*. Lanham, MD: Rowman & Littlefield.

Mayberry, M., & Rose, E. C. (1999). *Meeting the challenge: Innovative feminist pedagogies in action*. New York: Routledge.

Mogadime, D. (2003). Contradictions in feminist pedagogy: Black women students' perspectives. *Resources for Feminist Research, 30*(1), 7-32.

Musil, C. M. (1992a). *The courage to question: Women's studies and student learning*. Washington, D.C: Association of American Colleges.

Musil, C. M. (1992b). *Students at the center: Feminist assessment.* Washington, D.C: Association of American Colleges.

Nawratil, G. (1999). Implications of computer-conferenced learning for feminist pedagogy and women's studies: A review of the literature. *Resources for Feminist Research, 27*(1), 73-107.

Roth, J. (2008). Blogging in the classroom: Technology, feminist pedagogy, and participatory learning. *Atlantis, 32*(2), 80-91.

Shrewsbury, C. (1993). Feminist pedagogy: An updated bibliography. *Women's Studies Quarterly, 21*(3/4), 148-160.

Shrewsbury, C. (1987). Feminist pedagogy: A bibliography. *Women's Studies Quarterly, 15*(3/4): 116-124.

Watson, G. C. (2008). Teaching note: Against from within: Finding feminist pedagogical spaces between academic institutional margins. *Feminist Teacher, 19*(1), 71-73.

Weiler, K. (1988). *Women teaching for change: Gender, class & power.* South Hadley, Mass: Bergin & Garvey Publishers.

Weiler, K. (2001). *Feminist engagements: Reading, resisting, and revisioning male theorists in education and cultural studies.* New York: Routledge.

Webb, D. (2010). Paulo Freire and "the need for a kind of education in hope." *Cambridge Journal of Education, 40*(4), 327-339.

Appendix A

Context 1: 50-minute one-shot session at the introductory level. A first year composition class writing their first research paper comes to the library for instruction. The class assignment allows students to choose their own topic for research. They need to use at least five secondary sources, and at least one of them has to be scholarly. The rest need to be at least considered credible. See Appendix B for sample worksheets.	
Outcomes:	Students will be able to: <ul><li>Evaluate an information need in order to determine an appropriate search strategy</li><li>Locate, access, and evaluate appropriate information sources in order to meet information needs.</li><li>Identify elements of the bibliographic record in order to read, interpret, and compose accurate citations in MLA style.</li><li>Investigate the gender differences in students' college experience in order to raise awareness of the role of sexism in higher education.</li></ul>
Curriculum:	Students will need to know: <ul><li>how to access and use library research tools</li><li>how to evaluate search results in terms of information need</li><li>how to evaluate information, especially websites, using defined criteria</li></ul>
Pedagogy:	Present students with a worksheet containing the following: Before you begin research, it is important to do some 'presearch.' Presearch involves thinking critically about your topic and

brainstorming a list of terms and concepts associated with your topic. This will arm you with the tools you need to conduct a successful search on your topic. For this class session, we will work on a shared topic. The skills we practice today can then be applied to your own research topic.

Take a few moments now to brainstorm keywords related to the topic of a *successful college experience*. How do you define success in college? What factors influence a student's success in college? What helps female students be successful? Are there any factors that help male students achieve? Think about these questions and list your keywords below.

Think/Pair/Share: (10 minutes)
For the above scenario, ask students to brainstorm alone, and then brainstorm with a partner, and then call on students to share with the class. When monitoring the sharing portion of this activity, take care to validate students' responses, even if they do not seem to be on the right track, then guide them back to the original problem they were asked to address. Also during the sharing part, it might be useful to ask guiding questions to help students understand what distinguishes library searching from internet searching. After several keywords have been identified and written on the board, for example, the instructor can ask the class what the next step in the research process is. Inevitably, someone will suggest doing a Google search. At this point, ask the class why they think library searching is different than Google searching and why they are they are there in the library that day.

Student-led Demonstration: (15 minutes)

Ask for two student volunteers to conduct database demonstration. If no one volunteers, choose two students at from the roster or some other random method. The librarian will describe the characteristics and features of two or three relevant databases and the student volunteers will select which one to search. The first volunteer will be tasked with sitting at the instructor station computer and conducting a search in a database. The second volunteer will instruct and guide the first volunteer in locating articles on the class topic, providing the searcher with keywords generated during the Think/Pair/Share activity. Let the student volunteers guide the demonstration, but point out anything that you want the students to know if it does not come up organically during the demo. If there are certain key points that you want to make sure the students address, but you do not want to be too directive, you might include those on the worksheet and ask the students to use those as guidelines. For example, make sure evaluating information sources is addressed during the demonstration. Ask for input from the class regarding what makes a source credible and ask for a third volunteer to take notes on the board. Also make sure to that students are able to point out elements of the bibliographic record as a way of talking about source documentation and plagiarism prevention. You can also ask at this point, if it doesn't come up on its own during the student demonstration, how research tools are accessible from off campus.

Hands-on Individual Searching: (15 minutes)

After the student volunteers have completed a successful demonstration, allow students to have individual time to search on their own on their own topics. Students may also search for websites during this time using the criteria for credibility developed

	in the previous activity. Walk around the class, check on the students, and guide, encourage, and support students as indicated.
Assessment:	Informal observation of quality of responses during think/pair/share.
	Informal observation of quality of student searching during demonstration and during individual search time.
	Web-based multiple-choice knowledge test: (5-10 minutes) Students respond to a four question multiple choice knowledge test that asks students to identify the best place to start a research project, indicate whether library resources are available from off campus, identify which criteria to use for evaluating quality and credibility of sources, and determine whether a described scenario constitutes plagiarism.
Criteria:	If students are able to navigate a library database and locate at least one relevant article on the class topic, or on their own topic, I will know they have done this well. If student responses to the knowledge test are mostly correct, I will know they have done this well.

What makes this session feminist?

- Use of think/pair/share supports team problem-solving
- Use of consciousness-raising about gender differences in sample topic
- Student-led demonstration promotes an anti-hierarchical learning environment
- Student-led definition of terms supports collective knowledge production and creation
- Individual searching time empowers students and encourages active, hands-on learning

Context 2: 60 minute one-shot for a first year seminar American history course. The assignment requires them to use credible library sources to learn biographical information about the early American presidents and to define key terms relevant to that time period. See Appendix B for sample worksheets.	
Outcomes:	Students will be able to: • Evaluate an information need in order to determine an appropriate search strategy • Identify and select appropriate sources of information in order to demonstrate awareness of the variety and scope of information resources available to them • Navigate the library website in order to access and use library information sources • Identify a female historical figure in order to increase awareness of women throughout history
Curriculum:	Students will need to know: • how to access and use library research tools • how to evaluate search results in terms of information need • how to evaluate information, especially websites, using defined criteria
Pedagogy:	**The Time Machine Scenario: (10 minutes)** For a history class, this is a fun opportunity to introduce students to a female historical figure from the time period and region being studied in the course. This scenario also helps student achieve the second learning outcome: demonstrating awareness of the resources the library has to offer. Provide students with a scenario that has an historical figure of your choice arriving in the library

classroom in the present day. This figure is interested in learning about the contemporary library and what it has to offer compared to the libraries of her day. For example:

> Imagine the following scenario: Martha Washington, our nation's first First Lady, entered a time machine in the year 1789, and arrived in Room 235 of the Library at IU Southeast in the year 2011. Lady Washington, as she was referred to at the time, is rather surprised to find herself in a college classroom in the year 2011, and after you greet her and welcome her to IU Southeast, you learn that Lady Washington is interested in how people interact and communicate in the 21th century. She's especially interested in the way libraries have changed since the 18th century. There was no such thing as computers, the Internet, online article databases, or anything of the kind in her time. What would you tell Lady Washington about today's library? What kinds of resources does the library have to offer? Take a few minutes to brainstorm responses to this scenario, and talk with your neighbor to share ideas. Be prepared to share with the class how you would enlighten Lady Washington on the wonders of today's library!

Give students five minutes to work in pairs to respond to the questions, and then spend five minutes discussing as a group their responses. The key is to have them identify the various reasons why the library is an important resource.

Individual Searching (20 minutes)

Present students with the next step: having them explore the library resources they just identified as important:

> Now that you've informed Lady Washington about everything the library has to offer, you're going to put those library resources to work. This task will help you complete your library assignment for this class. You can use any of the following research tools: Biography in Context, Britannica, Credo Reference, and Gale Virtual Reference Library. These tools are accessible from the Article and Database Search page on the Library Homepage.
>
> 1. Conduct a search on one of your assigned presidents. Which research tool did you select? What keywords and search phrase did you use?
> 2. Choose *one* search result that is relevant to your topic. How do you access the article? (Is it right there on the page? Do you have to click on another link to access it?)
> 3. Is this a reliable source? How can you tell?

4. How would you use this source for your assignment for this class?

Group Discussion and Demonstration (20 minutes)

Ask for two student volunteers. The first volunteer will take notes on the board during the group discussion. Ask students to share their responses to the questions on their worksheet. Focus in particular on the question concerning reliability and how the source might be used in the class. Let the class

	come up with their own definition of reliability and help them refine it as needed. Then ask a second volunteer to demonstrate how to use one of the research tools used during the previous activity.
Assessment:	Informal observation of quality of responses during the Time Machine exercise.
	Informal observation of quality of student searching during demonstration and during individual search time.
	Web-based minute paper/muddiest point paper: (5-10 minutes) Take a few moments to think about the library session you attended today. Please tell us the following: 1. What did you learn today? 2. What interested you, surprised you, or made you curious? 3. What confused or frustrated you? 4. What will you do differently now that you've attended today's session? If time permits, the librarian instructor should try to address in class the responses to question #3. If time does not allow, provide a space for students to input their email address so that the librarian can respond to student feedback on that question.
Criteria:	If students are able to successfully identify key library resources and demonstrate how to use them, I'll know they've done this well. If students report that they learned something new about the library and its resources in the web-based survey, I'll know they have done this well.

What makes this session feminist?
- Use of consciousness-raising about female historical figures
- Student-led demonstration promotes an anti-hierarchical learning environmentStudent-led definition of criteria

- supports collective knowledge production and creation
- Individual searching time empowers students and encourages active, hands-on learning
- Assessment instrument that fosters reflection and addresses affective dimension of learning

Context 3: 50-75 minute one-shot for a discipline-specific class. This is a senior seminar class for psychology majors. Their class assignment is an 8-10 page research paper written in APA style. All sources must be scholarly journal articles or monographs. No websites are permitted. See Appendix B for sample worksheets.

Outcomes:	Students will be able to: • Identify and articulate information need or problem in order to develop a research plan appropriate to the investigative methods in the discipline. • Use discipline-appropriate controlled vocabulary, keywords, synonyms, and related terms in order to construct a search query. • Interpret bibliographic information in order to retrieve and locate sources and demonstrate ability to use appropriate attribution and documentation. • Describe the connection between domestic violence and women with PTSD in order to examine the impact of violence on women
Curriculum:	Students will need to know: • how to access and use relevant library research tools • how to construct a search query • how to evaluate search results in terms of information need • how to read a citation
Pedagogy:	**Read an article: (5-10 minutes)** Provide students with a copy of a brief popular press article about psychological study and ask them to read it. Choose an article that is related to gender or women in some way. I have previously used an article about a study investigating the connection between domestic violence and PTSD.

Whichever article you choose, make sure that it is something that is easy to track down in the scholarly literature. Avoid placing too many obstacles in the students' path.

Identify key features of article: (10 minutes)
In pairs, have students identify key elements of article as specified on the worksheet. For example, have them work together to find the study authors, study topic, relevant keywords, journal title, and article date.

Locate article: (15 minutes)
Ask students to work with a partner using library resources – particularly the Journals A-Z list—to locate full text of original study in scholarly format. They may need some assistance in using this tool. If it appears that students are struggling, ask one volunteer to come up to the instructor's workstation and guide them in demonstrating how to use the tool.

Locate additional sources: (20 minutes)
Ask students to locate at least one scholarly article and one monograph on the same topic as the original study using an article database and library catalog. Students can work alone or in pairs on this task using the keywords identified earlier. If students need help navigating to the psychology databases or the library catalog, ask for a knowledgeable volunteer to demonstrate this on the instructor workstation or to go around to each student and help him or her individually. A worksheet with guiding questions might be helpful here if there are certain key features you want to make sure students understand. For example, you might ask students to explore the bibliographic record and its hyperlinked subject terms as a way of helping

	them understand how controlled vocabulary searching works. **Demonstration (time permitting)** Ask one student to demonstrate for class how they completed the previous task.
Assessment:	Informal observation of quality of student responses and searching during demonstration and during individual search time. **One-sentence summary: (5-10 minutes)** Ask students to summarize what they learned in the library session in one sentence on an index card or using a web-based survey tool. Go around the room and ask students to read their sentences aloud.
Criteria:	If students are able to identify and locate the original scholarly article and additional sources on the same topic, I will know they have done this well. If students report that their library research skills have in some way been changed or enhanced by the session, I will know they have done this well.

What makes this session feminist?
- Use of think/pair/share supports team problem-solving
- Use of consciousness-raising about gender-related topic
- Student-led demonstration promotes an anti-hierarchical learning environment
- Student-led definition of criteria supports collective knowledge production and creation
- Assessment instrument fosters reflection.

Context 4: 50-75 minute one-shot. An intermediate-level class for nursing students just beginning the coursework for the major. Students have to research a nursing-related topic and prepare a ten-item annotated bibliography. Acceptable sources include scholarly articles, monographs, and credible websites, such as government agency sites. See Appendix B for sample worksheets.	
Outcomes:	Students will be able to: • Identify and articulate information need or problem in order to develop a research plan appropriate to the investigative methods in the discipline. • Use discipline-appropriate controlled vocabulary, keywords, synonyms, and related terms in order to construct a search query. • Locate, access, and evaluate appropriate information sources in order to meet information needs. • Describe the gendered nature of the nursing profession in order to identify the sexism and inequity inherent in the field.
Curriculum:	Students will need to know: • how to access and use relevant library research tools • how to construct a search query • how to evaluate search results in terms of information need • how to read a citation
Pedagogy:	**Comparing library and web-native information sources and tools (10 minutes):** Provide students with the Information Sources Chart in Appendix. White out the "information tools" boxes on the chart and have students work in pairs to try to fill those boxes in.

Demonstrating library and web-native information sources and tools (5 minutes):
On instructor's computer station, project the image of the Information Sources Chart and ask volunteers to provide feedback on how to fill in empty boxes.

Information searching teamwork: (20 minutes)
Divide class into teams of three students each. For example, if 24 students are in the class, there will be eight teams of three. Three of the teams will work on scholarly sources. Three of the teams will work on book sources. And the final two teams will work on web-native sources. Ask each team to conduct a search on a group-selected relevant topic to their coursework. Each team will need to find one relevant source that could be used for the annotated bibliography. Allow five minutes for explanation of the task and breaking into groups and then 15 minutes for searching. Provide students with topic: gender, pay equity, and the nursing profession.

Information searching teamwork demonstration: (20 minutes)
One team from each category will present and demonstrate their research findings to the class. Each team will be asked to describe what makes their search results relevant or appropriate to the assignment. The team in charge of searching the web will lead the class in a discussion of what makes web sources credible and reliable.

Individual search time (time permitting)
After the student volunteers have completed a successful demonstration, allow students to have individual time to search on their own on their own topics. Walk around the class, guide, encourage, and support students as indicated.

Assessment:	Informal observation of quality of student searching during demonstration and during individual search time. **Web-based defining features matrix (5-10 minutes)** This assessment instrument asks students to distinguish among the characteristics of scholarly, popular, and web-based information.
Criteria:	If students are able to successfully locate sources on their topic, I will know they have done this well. If the responses to the defining features matrix indicate that students understand the difference between the scholarly, popular, and web-based information, I will know they have done this well.

What makes this session feminist?
- Use of consciousness-raising about gender-related topic
- Student-led demonstration promotes an anti-hierarchical learning environment
- Student-led definition of criteria supports collective knowledge production and creation
- Teamwork facilitates the development of communication and problem-solving skills

Context 5: 50-75 minute one-shot for a graduate-level business course. Their class assignment is a 15-20 page research paper written in APA style. All sources must be scholarly journal articles or monographs. No websites are permitted. See Appendix B for sample worksheets.

Outcomes:	Students will be able to: • Identify and articulate information need or problem in order to develop a research plan appropriate to the investigative methods in the discipline. • Use discipline-appropriate controlled vocabulary, keywords, synonyms, and related terms in order to construct a search query. • Interpret bibliographic information in order to retrieve and locate sources and demonstrate ability to use appropriate attribution and documentation. • Describe sexist aspects of the corporate world in order to identify how employment discrimination affects women.
Curriculum:	Students will need to know: • how to access and use relevant library research tools • how to construct a search query • how to evaluate search results in terms of information need • how to read a citation
Pedagogy:	**Walking through the research process demo (15 minutes):** Ask a volunteer to go to the board and demonstrate for the class how to think through a research topic. Provide students with worksheets that explain how to formulate a research question, think about what kinds of sources are needed, where to find these sources, generating keywords, and come up with possible search queries. Guide students

	toward appropriate subject-specific tools if the students cannot identify them themselves. Facilitate the keyword brainstorming and search query construction in a way that validates student input while also refining student knowledge into something that is workable and likely to be successful. Provide students with a sample topic: women and the "glass ceiling" in business professions.
	Walking through the research process individual work (5 minutes) After working through one student's topic on the board, ask students to complete worksheet individually.
	Database searching demonstration and source evaluation discussion: (20 minutes) Ask a volunteer to demonstrate how to use an article database and the library catalog, searching on his or her own topic. Ask the rest of class to provide guidance and feedback for student as he or she conducts the search. Use a worksheet with guiding questions to facilitate discovery of advanced features of the database, such as controlled vocabularies, if relevant and appropriate to discussion. Ask the class to collectively determine the best sources in the search results, making sure to address what exactly makes those sources the best.
	Individual search time (time permitting) After the student volunteers have completed a successful demonstration, allow students to have individual time to search on their own on their own topics. Walk around the class, check on the students, and guide, encourage, and support students as indicated.
Assessment:	Informal observation of quality of student searching during demonstration and during individual search time.

	Web-based defining features matrix (5-10 minutes) This assessment instrument asks students to distinguish between the characteristics of article databases and the library catalog.
Criteria:	If students are able to successfully locate scholarly sources on their topic, I will know they have done this well. If the responses to the defining features matrix indicate that students understand the difference between the library catalog and article databases, I will know they have done this well.

What makes this session feminist?

- Use of consciousness-raising about gender-related topic
- Student-led demonstration promotes an anti-hierarchical learning environment
- Student-led definition of criteria supports collective knowledge production and creation

Appendix B

Sample Worksheet for Context 1 in Appendix A

Before you begin research, it is important to do some "presearch." Presearch involves thinking critically about your topic and brainstorming a list of terms and concepts associated with your topic. This will arm you with the tools you need to conduct a successful search on your topic. For this class session, we will work on a shared topic. The skills we practice today can then be applied to your own research topic.

Take a few moments now to brainstorm keywords related to the topic of a *successful college experience*. How do you define success in college? What factors influence a student's success in college? What helps female students be successful? Are there any factors that help male students achieve? Think about these questions and list your keywords below.

Next, turn to your neighbor and continue brainstorming. Write your responses to these questions here.

Sample Worksheet for Context 2 in Appendix A

Part 1: Imagine the following scenario: Martha Washington, our nation's first First Lady, entered a time machine in the year 1789, and arrived in Room 235 of the Library at IU Southeast in the year 2011. Lady Washington, as she was referred to at the time, is rather surprised to find herself in a college classroom in the year 2011, and after you greet her and welcome her to IU Southeast, you learn that Lady Washington is interested in how people interact and communicate in the 21th century. She's especially interested in the way libraries have changed since the 18th century. There was no such thing as computers, the Internet, online article databases, or anything of the kind in her time. What would you tell Lady Washington about today's library? What kinds of resources does the library have to offer? Take a few minutes to brainstorm responses to this scenario, and talk with your neighbor to share ideas. Be prepared to share with the class how you would enlighten Lady Washington on the wonders of today's library!

Part 2: Now that you've informed Lady Washington about everything the library has to offer, you're going to put those library resources to work. This task will help you complete your library assignment for this class. You can use any of the following research tools: **Biography in Context, Britannica, Credo Reference,** and **Gale Virtual Reference Library**. These tools are accessible from the **Article and Database Search** page on the Library Homepage.

Source #1

5. Conduct a search on one of your assigned **presidents**. Which research tool did you select? What keywords and search phrase did you use?

6. Choose *one* search result that is relevant to your topic. How do you access the article? (Is it right there on the page? Do you have to click on another link to access it?)

7. Is this a reliable source? How can you tell?

8. How would you use this source for your assignment for this class?

Source #2

1. Conduct a search on one of your assigned **key terms**. Which research tool did you select? What keywords and search phrase did you use?

2. Choose *one* search result that is relevant to your topic. How do you access the information source? (Is it right there on the page? Do you have to click on another link to access it?)

3. Is this a reliable source? How can you tell?

How would you use this source for your assignment for this class?

Sample Worksheet for Context 3 in Appendix A

Today you will do an activity designed to help you be able to:

- Identify and articulate information need or problem in order to develop a research plan appropriate to the investigative methods in the discipline.
- Use discipline-appropriate controlled vocabulary, keywords, synonyms, and related terms in order to construct a search query.
- Interpret bibliographic information in order to retrieve and locate sources and demonstrate ability to use appropriate attribution and documentation.
- Describe the connection between domestic violence and women with PTSD in order to examine the impact of violence on women

What does this mean in ordinary language?

1. Well, first of all, you are going to read the attached article.
2. Next, you will locate clues in the article that point to the original source of the study the article discusses. Can you find the journal title? One of the study's investigators? What keywords would you use to describe this article?
3. Next, you will use the Library's Full-text Journals A-Z List to find out our library's holdings for this journal; that is, you're going to find out what the library owns and where those materials are located.
4. Using the information you found via Full-text Journals A-Z List, find a copy of the original article cited in this cnn.com article.
5. For your next trick, you will review the bibliography of this original study, and following the same steps above, you will use Full-text Journals A-Z List to locate one article cited in the bibliography.

You will have 15 minutes to complete the above steps on your own. Then we will discuss as a group what you did, what you found, and how these skills you've just practiced might be useful for you beyond today's activity.

Ask for help if you need it—I'm here to be the guide on the side!

Sample Worksheet for Context 4 in Appendix A

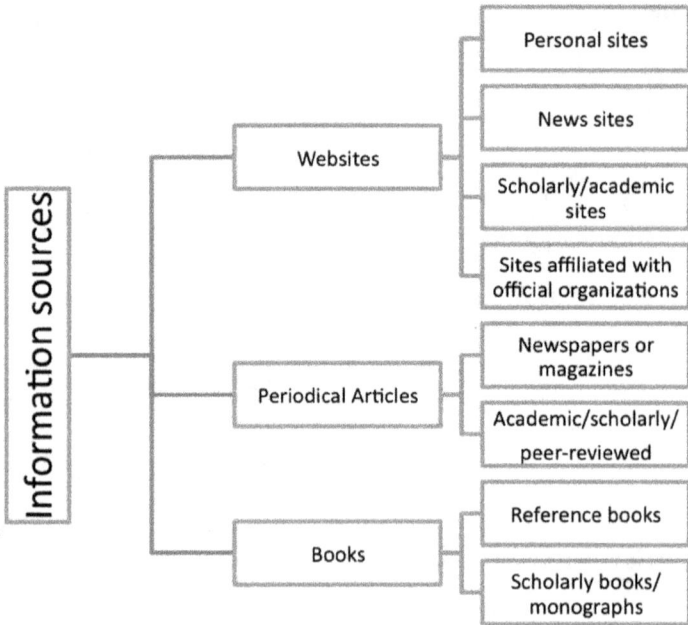

Your available research tools include: the library catalog, article databases, reference databases, and web search engines. Which tools will you use for each information source type?

Sample Worksheet for Context 5 in Appendix A

Part 1:   Thinking about your topic and preparing to search

Step 1:
What is your topic? Briefly state your topic in a sentence or two.

Step 2:
What kind of information sources do you need? Think in terms of **type** (scholarly articles, background information, magazine articles, newspaper articles, statistics or other facts/data, etc.) and in terms of **quality** (authority, currency, accuracy, reliability, etc.). Think also about **quantity**: how much information do you need (lots of articles? A few books? One encyclopedia article for background information?). List the kind of information sources you want, and how much you want, here.

Step 3:
What kind of information tools can you use to find the kinds of information sources you need? Which tool is the most appropriate tool for your specific information needs? For example, do you need a database that finds articles in specific subject areas, or would a more general, multi-disciplinary database be appropriate? List the tools you want to use here.

Step 4:

Once you've decided on the type of sources you want and the tools you have to locate them, **you need to formulate your search query.** Databases do not speak the same language we do, so you have to take your topic, boil it down to its bare bones, and then put it back together in database language. The first step of this is brainstorm a list of words and concepts associated with your topic. List those words here.

Step 5:

Then, using the words you just listed, **put those words together in a phrase**, using the word AND to connect them. Use quotation marks around terms you want to search as exact phrases. This is your search query.

Example of a weak search query:

the influence of media on body image and eating disorders

Example of a better search query:

media and "body image" and "eating disorders"

Formulate a few search queries and list them here.

Part 2: Searching for information on your topic

Step 1:
Using the search queries you came
up with on the previous page, conduct searches in one of the article
databases you identified to locate
articles on your topic. If you do not
get any results, try rephrasing your
search using the list of words you
generated on the previous page. List the search queries you
used here.

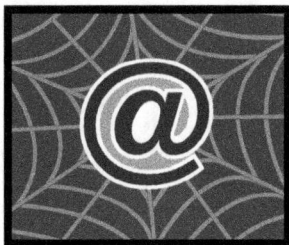

Step 2:
Review the first few search results by reading the titles, ab-
stracts, and subject headings of each citation. How can this
information be useful to you at this stage of your research?
What clues are available to help you determine quality, credibility, and relevance to your information need?

Step 3:
Experiment with the search limiters available (e.g. limit by
date range, full-text only, etc.) and conduct a new search.
How do these limiters affect your search results?

Step 4:
Try using AND to add in another search term. For example,
if your initial query was **media and "body image" and
"eating disorders"**, try **media and "body image" and
"eating disorders" and adolescents**. What additional term
did you use, and how did the addition of this term affect your
search results?

Step 5:

Choose one relevant article from your search results. How did you determine its relevance? Can you use any of this information to conduct new searches?

Appendix C

Sample Classroom Assessment Techniques

Defining Features Matrix Combined with One Sentence Summary

1. Choose which type of periodical this characteristic best describes:

		Scholarly Periodical	Popular Periodical
a)	Contains lengthy research articles on specialized topics.		
b)	Articles are written by scholars, experts, or professionals in an academic or scholarly field.		
c)	Usually the most appropriate information source for most kinds of formal academic research.		
d)	The intended audience of this periodical is a general, average, non-expert population.		

2. Please describe in your own words a) what you learned today, and b) how well you think you grasped the material.

Knowledge Test Combined with Muddiest Point

1. Choose the sentence that best explains the concept of using AND in an article database.
   a. The word AND limits, narrows, or decreases search results by joining two different concepts in a keyword search.
   b. The word AND increases search results by joining two different concepts in a keyword search.
2. In your own words, describe one concept addressed today that remains unclear to you on the next page. Please provide your email address if you'd like a librarian to follow up with you with an answer.

Knowledge Test Combined with One Minute Paper

1. Gertrude found a magazine article through Academic Search Premier. She copied a few sentences from the article and pasted those sentences into her research paper. She then turned in the paper without indicating in any way that she copied those sentences from anywhere else. Gertrude did not think there was anything wrong with this, but her friend Septimus disagreed. Who is right?
   a. Gertrude is right, because it doesn't matter if you only copy a few sentences. It would be a big deal if it were a whole paper, or a several paragraphs, but since she just took a few sentences, she didn't do anything wrong.
   b. Septimus is right, because you have to document a source somewhere in your paper, no matter how little of the source you used. It is considered plagiarism if you don't document that you used someone else's words or ideas.

2. Describe one thing you'll STOP doing as a result of today's library session.

3. Describe one think you'll START doing as a result of today's library session.

Knowledge Test Combined with One Minute Paper

1. You are working on a research paper about the ecological impact of the local food movement. Those who ascribe to this movement try to eat food that was grown and harvested locally, usually within a 100 mile radius. Many local food devotees, or "locavores," grow their own food, or shop at farmers' markets. Locavores are concerned with sustainable agriculture, the environmental impact of producing food, and eating foods that are in season.

   Here are some keywords you've brainstormed on your topic.

   - local food
   - locavores
   - farmers' markets
   - sustainable agriculture
   - ecological impact

Which of the following search phrases is the best phrase to use when conducting a keyword search on your topic?

    ○   eating locally

    ○   shopping at farmers' markets

    ○   local food AND ecological impact

    ○   local food AND locavores

2. If you had to describe how you feel about today's learning experience using only five words, what words would you choose?

Defining Features Matrix Combined with Muddiest Point

1. Choose which type of library research tool this characteristic best describes.

	Library Catalog	Article Database
IUCAT is an ex-ample of this kind of tool.	◉	○
The tool that al-lows you to search for articles in scholarly and popular periodicals.	○	◉
The tool that tells you what books and journals the library owns.	◉	○
The tool you use to have items sent to you from another IU library.	◉	○
Academic Search Premier is an ex-ample of this kind of tool	○	◉

2. In your own words, describe one concept addressed to-
    day that remains unclear to you, and how it makes you
    feel to still feel unclear about this concept Please provide
    your email address if you'd like a librarian to follow up
    with you with an answer.

Index

About the Author

Maria T. Accardi is Associate Librarian and Coordinator of Instruction at Indiana University Southeast in New Albany, Indiana, a regional campus in the IU system, located across the Ohio River from Louisville, Kentucky. She is a co-editor of *Critical Library Instruction: Theories and Methods* (Library Juice Press, 2010). She holds a BA in English from Northern Kentucky University, an MA in English from the University of Louisville, and an MLIS from the University of Pittsburgh. Prior to her career in librarianship, she worked in the college textbook publishing industry, taught and tutored first year college composition, and served as an indexer for a database company. She lives in Louisville.